103 Hikes
IN SOUTHWESTERN
BRITISH COLUMBIA
Third Edition

MARY AND DAVID MACAREE

Douglas & McIntyre
Vancouver /Toronto

The Mountaineers
Seattle

Published in Canada by
Douglas & McIntyre Ltd.
1615 Venables Street
Vancouver, British Columbia V5L 2H1

Canadian Cataloguing in Publication Data

Macaree, Mary.
    103 hikes in southwestern British Columbia

    Authors' names in reverse order in first edition.
    Includes index.
    ISBN 0-88894-546-9

    1. Hiking - British Columbia - Guide-books.
    2. British Columbia - Description and travel -
    1950-   - Guide-books. I. Macaree, David.
    II. British Columbia Mountaineering Club.
    III. Title.
    GV199.44.C22B753 1980   917.11'044   C80-091130-X

Published in the United States by The Mountaineers
306 2nd Avenue West, Seattle, WA 98119

Library of Congress Cataloguing in Publication Data

Macaree, Mary.
    103 hikes in southwestern British Columbia.

    First ed. (1973) by D. Macaree.
    Includes index.
    1. Hiking - British Columbia - Guide books.
    2. British Columbia - Description and travel -
    Guide-books. I. Macaree, David, joint author.
    II. Macaree, David. 103 hikes in southwestern
    British Columbia. III. British Columbia Mountain-
    eering Club. IV. Title.
    GV199.44.C22B746 1980   917.11'04'4   80-17573
    ISBN 0-89886-140-3

Unless otherwise credited, all photos by Mary Macaree
Cover photo of Crown Mountain (Hike 4) by Mary Macaree
Design by Marge Mueller
Maps by Mary Macaree
Typeset by The Typeworks
Printed and bound in Canada by D.W. Friesen & Sons Ltd.

CONTENTS

Page

Page

INTRODUCTION 6

NORTH SHORE
1   Black Mountain 10
2   Howe Sound Crest Trail .. 12
3   Hollyburn and Strachan .. 14
4   Goat Mountain 16
5   Mount Fromme 18
6   Lynn Headwaters 20
7   Lynn Peak 22
8   Mount Seymour 24
9   Elsay Lake 26
10 Three-Chop Trail 29

HOWE SOUND
11 Sunset Trail 32
12 Unnecessary Mountain .. 34
13 Lions Trail 36
14 Mount Harvey 38
15 Brunswick Mountain 40
16 Deeks Lakes 42
17 Deeks Peak 44
18 Mount Capilano 46
19 Petgill Lake 48
20 Stawamus Chief 50
21 Stawamus Squaw 52

SECHELT AND ISLANDS
22 Mount Roderick 54
23 Mount Gardner 56
24 Mount Artaban 60
25 Gambier Island West 62
26 Lesser Mount Steele 64
27 Galiano Island 66

SQUAMISH-CHEAKAMUS
28 Elfin Lakes 68
29 Mamquam Lake 70
30 High Falls Creek 72
31 Alice Ridge 74
32 Garibaldi Lake 76
33 Panorama Ridge 78
34 Black Tusk 80
35 Empetrum Peak 82

36 Brew Lake 84
37 Brandywine Meadows ... 86
38 Helm Creek Trail 88

WHISTLER
39 Rainbow Lake 90
40 Alpine Whistler 92
41 Russet Lake 94
42 Wedgemount Lake 96

PEMBERTON
43 Tenquille Lake 98
44 Tenquille Creek 100
45 Place Glacier Trail 102
46 Joffre Lakes 104
47 Blowdown Creek 106
48 Lizzie Creek 108

FRASER VALLEY NORTH
49 Diez Vistas Trail 110
50 Lindsay Lake 112
51 Eagle Peak 114
52 Dilly-Dally Trail 116
53 Burke Ridge 118
54 Widgeon Lake 120
55 UBC Research Forest .. 122
56 Alouette Mountain 124
57 Golden Ears 126
58 Mount St. Benedict 128

HARRISON LAKE
59 Bear Mountain 130
60 Lookout Peak 132

FRASER VALLEY SOUTH
61 Sumas Mountain 134
62 Vedder Peak
    (West Trail) 136
63 Mount Thurston 138
64 Cheam Peak 140

CHILLIWACK RIVER
65 Mount Amadis
    (International Ridge) ... 142

CONTENTS (CONTINUED)

Page

Page

66 Liumchen Ridge 144
67 Mount MacFarlane 146
68 Mount Laughington 148
69 Williamson Lake 150
70 Mount Ford 152
71 Williams Ridge 154
72 Radium Lake 156
73 Greendrop Lake 158
74 Flora Lake 160

SILVER-SKAGIT
75 Eaton Lake 162
76 Skagit River Trail 164
77 Skyline Trail West 166
78 Galene Lakes 168

FRASER CANYON
79 Mount Lincoln 170
80 First Brigade Trail (1848) 172
81 Gate Mountain 174
82 Stein River Trail 176
83 Botanie Mountain 178

COQUIHALLA
84 The Needle 180
85 Zoa Peak 182

86 Thar Peak 184
87 Mount Henning 186
88 Mount Thynne 188
89 Stoyoma Mountain 190

HOPE-MANNING PARK
90 Mount Outram 192
91 Silverdaisy Mountain 194
92 Punch Bowl 196
93 Hope Pass 198
94 Poland Lake 200
95 Three Brothers
       Mountain 202
96 Lightning Lakes 204
97 Frosty Mountain 206
98 Skyline Trail East 208

KEREMEOS
99   Crater Mountain 210
100 Cathedral Lakes 212
101 Cathedral Rim 214
102 Lakeview Mountain 218
103 Keremeos Columns 220

ADDITIONAL HIKES 222
INDEX 223

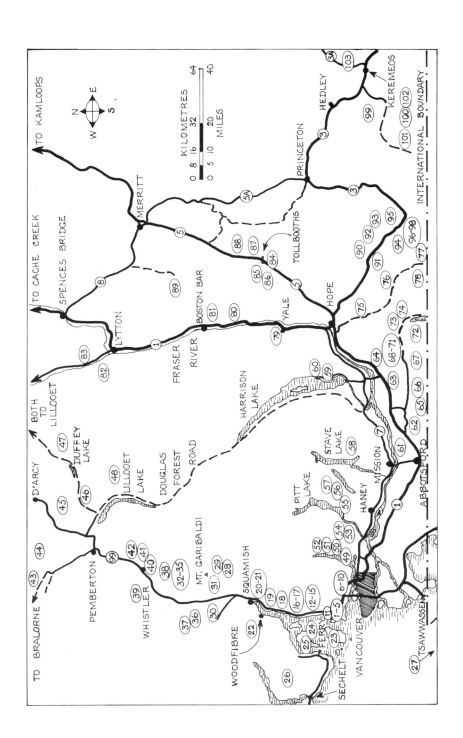

INTRODUCTION

This edition, the third, of **103 Hikes in Southwestern British Columbia** incorporates many features of its predecessors, the major difference being the removal of hikes on Vancouver Island and their replacement by outings in the area recently made more accessible to Lower Mainland hikers by the opening of Highway 5, with additions eastward along Highway 3 as well. The area now covered, therefore, stretches from a little beyond Pemberton to Lytton in the north, from Sechelt in the west to Keremeos in the east, and along the 49th parallel in the south. Rechecking of descriptions has led to some exclusions and a number of alterations, the result of highway improvements and industrial activity coupled with increased involvement in trail-building by organizations, both public and private, the latter development representing a considerable change from the state of affairs in 1973, when the first edition appeared under the auspices of the B.C. Mountaineering Club of Vancouver and the Mountaineers of Seattle.

Greater concern for the outdoors among hikers has also affected trails, with clubs helping to create and maintain them, marking them with the standard 4-cm squares of fluorescent orange aluminum tape in forests or with orange paint on rocky stretches. In such activities, umbrella groups such as the Outdoor Recreation Council and the Federation of Mountain Clubs of British Columbia have provided liaison with government agencies and defended hikers' interests. Ultimately, though, the responsibility for keeping tracks and routes in good order rests with you, the hiker. Please leave unsullied any area you visit by packing out your garbage; do your best to protect trails; do not cut corners and do obey signs; if backpacking, carry a stove to eliminate the need for a fire and use designated camping spots whenever possible. Heavy use of sensitive alpine terrain can destroy the delicate vegetation. In short, treat the environment gently.

As with all else in this imperfect world, trails are altered, sometimes for the better, more often for the worse. That is why it is impossible to guarantee that a few years after publication they will be as we have described them in this book. In the coastal forest, shrubs and fast-growing alder can quickly obliterate trails if they are not brushed out regularly. Flash flooding and high runoff levels may wash out bridges and make routes impassable. Trails are especially prone to erosion if their surfaces have already been damaged by off-road vehicles, including mountain bikes.

Like any other moderately strenuous outdoor activity, hiking involves a small element of risk, though most of the time you are probably safer—and a good deal healthier—on a mountain trail than on one of our city streets. Still, you should ensure that you are properly equipped and sufficiently experienced for the outing you are embarked on, preferably with someone who knows the area if it is unfamiliar to you. You should have with you the recommended essentials: sunglasses, small knife, matches in a waterproof case, fire-starter (candle or chemical), flashlight (checked from time to time), compass and map. You should carry also a first-aid kit, and extra

East from Eagle Peak: Coquitlam Mountain on the right (Hike 51)

clothing, food and liquid, the final items being necessary to protect against hypothermia (heat loss) or dehydration. Naturally, you will wear strong comfortable footwear (boots give more support and protection than shoes), suitable socks, and carry adequate rain gear. For early season hiking, you will need an ice-axe or pole to test your footing and to give you greater stability on hard snow.

Make sure that at least one responsible person is aware of your plans. Be ready to abandon a hike if it is tougher than you expected or if the weather turns bad. Check trail markers and don't try to second guess their direction. If you do lose sight of markers, backtrack to the last seen and start again. If lost, decide whether to stay where you are or try to return. Generally you should stop, but if you do decide to move, use your map and compass to establish points of reference and leave clear indications of your line of travel. For more information on this and related matters, you may obtain a pamphlet, **Hiking: A Guide to Safety in British Columbia,** from the Outdoor Recreation Council (1200 Hornby Street, Vancouver, B.C. V6Z 2E2, tel. 687-3333), a body that issues pamphlets on other aspects of outdoor recreation as well.

One good way to gain experience is to hike as a member of an organized party. Besides the B.C. Mountaineering Club (Box 2674, Vancouver, B.C. V6B 3W8) and the North Shore Hikers (Box 4355, Vancouver, B.C. V6B 4A1), the Lower Mainland boasts a number of other outdoor groups, details of which you may obtain from the Federation of Mountain Clubs of British Columbia (1200 Hornby Street, Vancouver, B.C. V6Z 2E2, tel. 687-3333) which also publishes various leaflets and sponsors training sessions in outdoor activities, both summer and winter.

Maps and guides for hikers are numerous. The 1:50,000 federal topographic map series covers the whole region. The Outdoor Recreation Council (ORC) has a series of recreation maps in a scale of 1:100,000 covering most of the areas included in this book. All of the foregoing are obtainable from Dominion Map Ltd. of 1104 West Broadway, Vancouver or from World Wide Books and Maps, 949 Granville Street, Vancouver, while the ORC maps are in regular bookstores as well. Among guides currently in print, some are more specialized than others. **The Best of B.C.'s Hiking Trails** by Bob Harris covers the whole province. Bruce F. Fairley's **Climbing and Hiking in Southwestern British Columbia** is essentially for climbers, though it does indicate approach routes; Roger and Ethel Freeman's **Exploring Vancouver's North Shore Mountains** gives a step-by-step account of that area, and Claude Roberge's **Hiking Garibaldi Park at Whistler's Back Door** deals with a similarly limited territory. Vancouver Island, likewise, has **Hiking Trails I, II** and **III** published by the Outdoor Club of Victoria.

For provincial parks, brochures prepared by the Parks and Outdoor Recreation Division may be obtained in tourist information offices or in the parks themselves. The Ministry of Forests and Lands publishes a series of **Forest Service Recreation Sites** which comprise fold-out maps and lists of sites and trails for each district. These you may get from the Vancouver Regional Office or from the appropriate district office.

Hiking often stimulates the development of ancillary interests also. If you have some curiosity in the natural manifestations around you, you may consider joining the Vancouver Natural History Society (Box 3021, Vancouver, B.C. V6B 3X5) or some similar body. If, however, you prefer to develop some expertise on your own, you may start with **Exploring the Outdoors: Southwestern B.C.** by Tony Eberts and Al Grass, which reflects the authors' interest in all aspects of nature, and go on to a general natural history such as Stephen Whitney's **A Field Guide to the West Coast Mountains,** following them up with one or other of the handbooks published by the British Columbia Provincial Museum and available from the Queen's Printer or from the Vancouver Museum, 1100 Chestnut Street. Among these are G. C. Earl's **Reptiles of British Columbia,** C. J. Guiget's **Birds of British Columbia** and Ian McTaggart-Cowan's **Mammals of British Columbia.** A more general guide for bird recognition is **Birds of North America** by Chandler Robbins and others. For the flora of the province, C. P. Lyons's **Trees, Shrubs and Flowers to Know in British Columbia** is

Bishop Glacier from Opal Cone (Hike 29)

a basic study. Then for the study of human settlement, **British Columbia Place Names** by G. P. V. and Helen Akrigg is a handy reference.

In **103 Hikes** itself each description includes the vehicle approach, a few points of natural or historical interest and an indication of what you may expect on each trail. A summary, as well as identifying the appropriate topographic map, gives in round terms the distance to be covered in kilometres and miles, the point of highest elevation and an indication of the difference between that and your starting height in metres and feet. When horizontal distances of less than a kilometre are supplied, they are given in metres only, as one yard is roughly equivalent to one metre. In addition, the appropriate map in the 1:50,000 series is identified; this is an essential supplement to the sketch map that accompanies each hike description. Finally, it may be noted that many of the trails described lend themselves to ski-touring or snowshoeing, and thus may be used throughout much of the year despite the recommended "Best" period.

In closing, the authors wish to express their gratitude to the many people whose assistance has helped in preparation of this guide. Members of the Provincial Parks and Outdoor Recreation Division, the Ministry of Forests and Lands and B.C. Hydro have answered questions and given advice. Friends and acquaintances have been helpful in meeting demands upon their time and patience, especially those who provided company and support on exploratory hikes. Ultimately, though, recognition has to be given to the trail blazers, those of a past generation like Walter Cadillac, some of whose fine photos enhance this book, and others of a more recent vintage like Paul Binkert and Halvor Lunden, the latter pair creators and improvers of trails par excellence. Nor should individual club members who have led or taken part in trail-clearing projects be forgotten. They have made possible much of the pleasure that you get from hiking in southwestern British Columbia.

1 BLACK MOUNTAIN

Round trip 16 km (10 mi)
Allow 7 hours
High point 1217 m (3992 ft)
Elevation gain 1067.5 m (3500 ft)
Best May to November
Map Vancouver North 92G/6

A steep but rewarding trail, with magnificent views over Howe Sound, leads to the alpine meadows and small lakes of the summit plateau. Although close to Vancouver and easily accessible, Black Mountain demands considerable expenditure of energy by those who ascend it from the west; the result, however, makes it worthwhile.

Follow Highway 1/99 west for 12 km (7.5 mi) from the traffic light at its Taylor Way access. Stay right for Squamish where the ferry traffic goes left and watch for the entry to a small parking space just before a yellow and black diagonally striped road sign on the right retaining wall.

From here the trail, an old road, rises steeply to a small pond beside which the Baden-Powell Trail enters from the right, some 20 minutes after its beginning at the top of Eagleridge Drive. Keep left and continue for about an hour passing watershed signs on your right. In its upper reaches the road becomes more and more washed out and is finally replaced by a trail that swings from northeast to east in pleasant open forest. Next you approach Nelson Creek, but before you reach it, you may notice a faint trail going off left. This was the old route to Black Mountain via Do-nut Rock; however, it is steep, bluffy and somewhat eroded, so it is no longer popular. If you do decide to use it, you should do so on the ascent, despite its steepness, for the descent can be tricky.

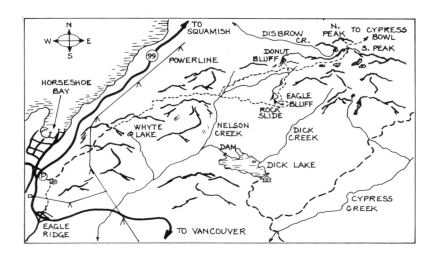

View over Howe Sound – *W. Cadillac*

The main trail crosses the creek and after a little longer in the forest it breaks into the open on the first talus slope that you have to negotiate. On the next rock slide the grade steepens, and your route is marked with paint splashes on rocks or by poles as you approach Eagle Bluff at 1094 m (3500 ft). You will surely want to savour the views from here (and get your breath back) as you look south along the coast of Georgia Strait and west to Vancouver Island. In fact, if you do this hike in early summer, this may well be your destination, for snow lies long on the Black Plateau and the going may be tedious.

As you continue to the peak(s) the trail undulates by picturesque little lakes until you reach a fork, the left being the route to Black Mountain. The south peak is reached first in a series of switchbacks, while the north (inexplicably signed "Yew Lake Lookout") lies beyond, past a small lake in the hollow between. From either peak the view is panoramic with the great snowfield of the Tantalus Range in the northwest, the dome of Mount Baker in the southeast and Vancouver below.

If you wish to vary your return trip and have been able to organize transportation, a crossover ending at the downhill ski area in Cypress Provincial Park is possible and reduces the walking time by nearly two hours. To do this, watch for the Baden-Powell Trail going right (east) in the pass between the peaks and follow it down.

2 HOWE SOUND CREST TRAIL (SOUTH)

Round trip 18 km (11.3 mi)
Allow 7 hours
High point 1510 m (4950 ft)
Elevation gain 600 m (1950 ft)
Best July to October
Map Vancouver North 92G/6

It is always pleasant to record new hiking trails close to the city of Vancouver instead of the disappearance of old favourites in the face of "progress." Into this category falls the Howe Sound Crest Trail, a high-level route giving access from Cypress Provincial Park to Unnecessary Mountain and the West Lion with a partial continuation to Porteau via Deeks Lakes (Hike 16). Although incomplete, enough of it exists to give several satisfactory day hikes of which the following is an example.

This trail has something of a history: the present trail is a re-creation by UBC's Varsity Outdoor Club of part of the one-time route to the Lions before the days of a road along Howe Sound, when access even to Hollyburn and Mount Strachan was on foot from West Vancouver. Now the parking lot for the Cypress chairlifts is some 14 km (9 mi) into the valley of the creek that gives the provincial park its name. Some difference!

From the parking lot, walk westward along the signposted trail that forks right from Yew Lake Trail, then after crossing a roadway take a foot-trail angling uphill. This leads, via a small ravine and a stretch of upper road, to the untouched forest on the west side of Mount Strachan, from which point signs of human activity are few, and the cool forest gives you an idea of what the whole mountain used to be like.

Along the way you have glimpses of Howe Sound and Sechelt as you gradually turn east and follow the line of Montizambert Creek into an interesting meadow in the saddle north of Mount Strachan with a view to the

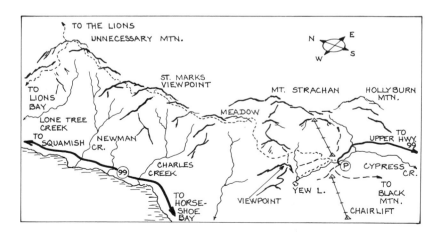

Northwest from St. Marks Summit

east over Lembke Creek as it drops to the Capilano watershed.

From here, follow the trail north along the ridge, negotiating one or two wooded knolls en route. About an hour beyond the meadow is St. Marks Summit, a possible destination with viewpoints on both sides of the trail just before it drops some 150 m (500 ft) into a col. It next climbs quite steeply the 350 m (1150 ft) back to crest level and goes over another two substantial bumps to Unnecessary Mountain, a satisfactory destination for a day hike. The trail, however, continues to the base of the West Lion, being joined en route by the trail from Lions Bay.

Return is normally by the same route unless you have managed to arrange for a pickup in Lions Bay village, either at the foot of the old Unnecessary Mountain Trail (Hike 12) or at the end of the "new" Lions Trail (Hike 13).

Lunch with jays on Hollyburn Peak

3 HOLLYBURN AND STRACHAN

Round trip 16 km (10 mi)
Allow 6 hours
High points
　　Hollyburn 1324 m (4345 ft)
　　Strachan 1454 m (4769 ft)
Elevation gain (total) 690 m (2250 ft)
Best July to October
Map Vancouver North 92G/6

Development of Cypress Provincial Park has put both these local summits within reach of a single day hike. Of course, you may double your pleasure by doing each one separately, using the cross-country ski area parking for Hollyburn and the downhill ski parking for Strachan.

To tackle both summits in one day, turn sharp right off the access road just beyond the powerline crossing and park near the Provincial Parks sign. Head uphill to the Hollyburn ridge crest and turn left along the ridge just beyond a skiers' warming hut immediately below Fourth Lake. From here walk the ridge, its colours spectacular in fall, and rise via a pleasant open meadow to the summit with its resident panhandling whiskey jacks.

To get to Mount Strachan (pronounced "Strawn") from here, look for the taped route dropping sharply from northeast of the summit into the pass between the two mountains, taking a little extra care on the steeper sections. Now you start rising again on a trail that parallels the big bend of the Collins Ski Run. The marked trail goes off right across an attractive meadow and into the trees, steepening in the process and passing a few pieces of aircraft wreckage. Finally you break out into the open and follow cairns north to the summit. When you reach the top, however, you realize that Mount Strachan has two summits with a dip of some 60 m (200 ft) between them. Both provide rewarding views: north along the connecting ridge to the Lions and the peaks beyond, west across Howe Sound to the mountains of Sechelt and east to Grouse Ridge, Goat Mountain and Crown, with Cathedral rising majestically behind.

To return, follow your outward route back to the pass between the mountains; this time, however, stay right to pick up the old trail that rounds the west shoulder of Hollyburn, joins the Baden-Powell Trail and brings you back to the ridge about 10 minutes' walk above the warming hut by Fourth Lake.

North from Mt. Strachan – *W. Cadillac*

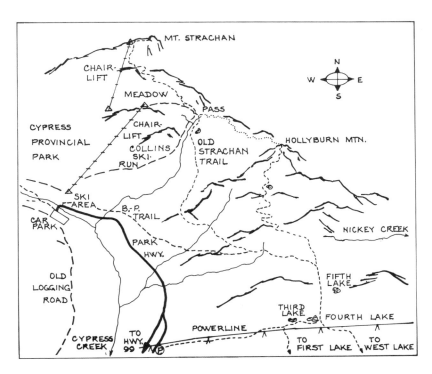

Crown Mountain from the summit— *W. Cadillac*

NORTH SHORE

4 GOAT MOUNTAIN

Round trip 17.5 km (11 mi)
Allow 8 hours
High point 1399 m (4587 ft)
Elevation gain 1067 m (3500 ft)
Best July to October
Map Vancouver North 92G/6

You may, if you wish, make this an easy hike by taking the Grouse Mountain Skyride to its upper terminal and setting out on foot from there. If, however, you want a more strenuous outing you may reach that point by hiking an upward extension of the old B.C. Mountaineering Club Trail (now part of the Baden-Powell Centennial Trail) that starts a little west of the one-time lower chairlift parking lot, reached by going east from Capilano Road on Montroyal Boulevard and turning left on Skyline Drive.

Park at the final bend where the trail goes off among trees along the west side of the mountain. Take the right (uphill) fork after about 10 minutes and cross two creeks, originally bridged by the efforts of the Boy Scouts. After about 40 minutes you see the site of an old cabin among the trees to your left, and it is here that you take the route (Larsen's Trail) that forks right and uphill. This ascends steadily, zigzagging upward towards the crest of the ridge where it forks again, this time the left being the appropriate choice (right goes to the ski village). Finally, as the grade eases, you meet a wider trail which you follow to the left, emerging just below the Alpine Cafeteria and possible refreshment.

From here, head around the west side of Grouse Peak, following the service road with its Watershed signs until you reach the col between Dam

Mountain and Grouse. Now you ascend the south slope of Dam, crossing and recrossing the waterpipe from Kennedy Lake, until at the eastern end of the second switchback you come on a new trail that takes you north round the mountain's east shoulder. The old summit bypass drops from the high point of the pipeline but the two reunite a little before a nice open viewpoint with a log to sit on. Next you rejoin the main ridge where you meet the trail over Dam's summit as you continue north, with Crown Mountain (watershed and out of bounds) across the valley to your left front.

Next the ridge narrows and becomes more open with, beyond Little Goat, a change of direction to the northeast, skirting the steep drop-off to Crown Pass. The minor trail, insignificant at present, dropping off left from the ridge's low point heads into the pass and will eventually be upgraded to provide a link via Hanes Creek with Lynn Headwaters Trail (Hike 6). The final ascent involves a little scrambling, and the inexperienced should be careful, especially when snow is on the ground. Goat Mountain summit is a steep-sided rocky knoll commanding fine views over the two nearby peaks of Crown Mountain—the Pyramid and the Camel—as well as of the mountains to north and east. These contrast vividly with the outlook over the city and the lower Fraser to the south.

The trail is not marked, but it is well defined and easy to follow, and except for a stretch between Dam and Grouse, it remains mainly on the ridge. Your return is by the same route as far as the ski area. From here, you may descend by the Cut ski slope to the old lower village, then follow the one-time chairlift right-of-way down to the parking lot, or alternatively, you may elect to ride down on the gondola and walk back southeast along the powerline to Skyline Drive and your vehicle.

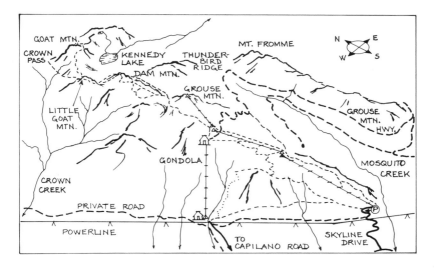

NORTH SHORE

5 MOUNT FROMME

Round trip 14.5 km (9 mi)
Allow 6 hours
High point 1177 m (3861 ft)
Elevation gain 854 m (2800 ft)
Best June to November
Map Vancouver North 92G/6

Here is a delightful close-in ramble with forest trails, the upper valley of Mosquito Creek, and the wooded slopes of your objective to provide variety as you climb. Even the vehicle approach is interesting, involving a drive north up Lonsdale in North Vancouver and a right turn onto Braemar followed by a left to St. George's Avenue. Next comes another right for one block on Tamarack, then a left on St. Mary's, with a steep rise followed by parking just to the left of the road on a powerline right-of-way.

After you park, walk west on the powerline for a short distance then veer right on a trail (the St. George's) which first crosses a clearing before entering the forest. As you proceed, your route is intersected by another trail, part of the Baden-Powell Centennial project. Continue upward; after some 40 minutes you reach the old Grouse Mountain Highway. Walk uphill on this to a sharp corner, at which point stay left, following an old logging road into the valley of Mosquito Creek.

This road heads for a creek crossing just below an interesting waterfall. Do not cross the creek; look for the taped route rising up the right-hand bank. This takes you into more trees and, eventually, to the old Grouse

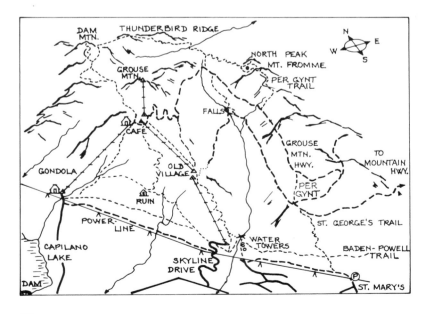

Small lake near the summit— *H. Lunden*

Mountain Highway once more. Stay with this as it heads for the upper creek crossing, but again stay right where the road swings back, picking up an old pipeline route that goes into trees on the north side of the creek, and follow it to a saddle.

Here, cast about to the right to find the marked route heading upward through the trees then along the west side of an attractive little lake a short distance below the main summit. Shortly before the lake, however, a trail has gone off left to what may be called the north peak, the view from which is better than that from its slightly higher neighbour to the south, itself reached by continuing around the lake and turning northeast. Of course, you may walk from one to the other, giving yourself views north, east and south. Returning, you may travel south on the Grouse Mountain Highway to a point about 60 metres beyond an old gravel pit where a new trail, the Per Gynt, drops downhill to emerge at the fork between the upper and lower roads.

Returning, drop eastward to the fork just below the peak and go left on a trail signed "Per Gynt." Follow this as it meanders through open forest then drops steeply downhill to emerge on the Grouse Mountain Highway. Travel south to a point on the right about 60 m beyond a gravel pit where the Per Gynt Trail resumes, descending to come out at the fork between the upper and lower roads.

View up Lynn Creek

NORTH SHORE

6 LYNN HEADWATERS

Round trip (to Lynn Creek crossing)
19 km (11.8 mi)
Allow 6 hours
High point 427 m (1400 ft)
Elevation gain 229 m (750 ft)
Best April to November
Map Vancouver North 92G/6

The new wilderness park in the upper valley of a creek that was until recently off-limits watershed provides hikers with a number of exciting possibilities once the upstream trail and its subsidiaries are complete. Indeed, strong hikers even now can make the crossover to Grouse Mountain via Hanes Creek and Crown Pass, although one major difficulty (the awkwardness of scree slopes aside) is the crossing of Lynn Creek at periods of high water.

To reach the park, follow Lynn Valley Road north, passing the turnoff to Lynn Canyon Park en route. Beyond Dempsey Road continue straight ahead on Intake Road, narrow and winding for about 1.5 km (1 mi) to a parking area at the entrance, from which you proceed on foot across the creek. Here you turn left on the counterclockwise branch of Lynn Loop Trail and follow the valley upstream, noting here and there evidence of past rampages where water has torn out stretches of road or covered it with rocks and gravel, the whole in contrast with the puny works of man as represented by abandoned bits of machinery with, at one point, a great tangle of wire and wooden staves, remains of the old pipes that once carried North Vancouver's water supply.

After 20 minutes or so, continue straight ahead where a steep connector to Headwaters Trail goes off right. Follow the creek on Cedars Mill Trail to a wide debris torrent where your track and the upper one come together again. Here is a pleasant spot for a brief rest, the last viewpoint from the trail, at least for the time being, since it exists mainly to give access to such proposed routes as the Hanes Creek/Crown Pass crossover, the approach to Coliseum Mountain via Norvan Creek, and an extension to Lynn Lake itself. Beyond this point, therefore, the main interest is in the forest itself, in the signs of bygone logging activity, the huge stumps, and the corduroy underpinnings of the old roads along which logs were moved on hard-tired trucks bearing little resemblance to today's monsters. Here and there, too, are the remains of cookhouses from long-ago logging camps.

Even after the trail—as constructed to official standards—ends (in 1988) at Norvan Creek, the going remains good to the Lynn Lake Trail turnoff 9.4 km (5.9 mi) from your start. Here you are close to the main creek, the tapes on its opposite side signalling the continuation (under construction) of the Crown Pass crossover. This entails a very long day with an elevation change of 1037 m (3400 ft) and an extra distance of 13 km (8 mi), somewhat less if you elect to ride down by the Skyride. Perhaps, therefore, return by your outward route is indicated, at least on a preliminary survey of what this nearby wilderness has to offer the city dweller.

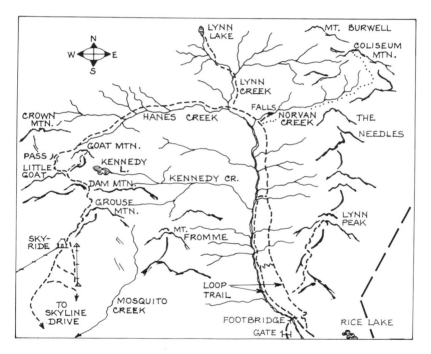

7 LYNN PEAK

Round trip 9.5 km (6 mi)
Allow 5 hours
High point 1010 m (3315 ft)
Elevation gain 825 m (2700 ft)
Best May to October
Map Vancouver North 92G/6

Travelling north across the Second Narrows Bridge, you look directly ahead at a well-timbered ridge rising between the valleys of Lynn Creek and the Seymour River. Well, your objective is the minor summit at its south end, one made possible by the creation of Lynn Headwaters Park, the entrance to which is your starting point.

This time, your crossing of Lynn Creek is followed by a right turn and a gradual rise on a wide gravel road for about 400 metres before you go sharp left on the Lynn Loop Trail that runs north along an upper bench. After about 10 minutes, you arrive at a washed out logging road on your right. This is your route (if you come to the remains of an old cabin on your left, you have gone too far). Stay on this track, marked with tapes, as you switchback up to the ridge and, shortly thereafter, to your first viewpoint, a somewhat restricted one, but giving an excuse for a rest as you look across the valley of the Seymour and southeast to the populated areas of Greater Vancouver.

Your next point of interest is a grove of stately trees, the so-called "Enchanted Forest", to be followed by an open area on the ridge's east side with a wider range of views than you had earlier. This clearing has an interesting history: it was the mooring station for the balloon used in a 1967 logging operation designed to salvage some of the timber damaged by Hurricane Frieda on slopes too steep for conventional methods. From here the trail turns uphill and makes a wide S-bend before resuming more or less its original direction in second-growth forest, the trees small and close-

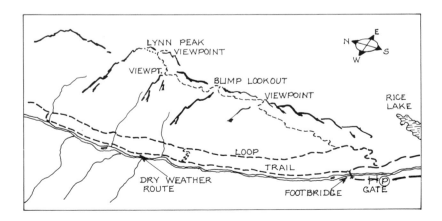

A giant slain

packed. It has been brushed out, however, and eventually you find yourself in large timber again as you rise steeply to the ridge crest which widens and flattens before you find yourself at the end of the cleared trail, a metal marker announcing the fact, though tapes do continue northward towards the peak. Your most rewarding destination lies a little south and to the right on an open bluff with a commanding view, the bridge across the harbour naturally being full in the centre of your field of vision, while to your left is the Seymour massif, southwest Burnaby Mountain, and, of course, the whole inner harbour in front of you.

On your return to the Loop Trail, consider turning right along the bench instead of tamely going back by your outward route. On your journey northward, you go through agreeable open forest with a possible side trip to some huge glacial erratics as an added attraction. Finally you descend the switchback trail and walk downstream along Lynn Creek to your starting point.

North from Mt. Seymour

NORTH SHORE

8 MOUNT SEYMOUR

Round trip 9 km (5.5 mi)
Allow 4 hours
High point (Third Peak) 1453 m
**   (4766 ft)**
Elevation gain 450 m (1475 ft)
Best July to October
Map Coquitlam 92G/7

Until a few years ago, the park authorities took little responsibility for routes on this mountain's upper slopes, leaving private groups to provide whatever marking was done. All that has changed, and a good trail now gives access to the third and highest peak of Mount Seymour, crossing en route a scenic subalpine area of meadows and rocky outcrops. And in addition to these attractive surroundings, the hiker has a wide range of views from lush lowlands to stark summits.

The trailhead is easily found near the chairlift station at the north end of the upper parking lot. At first it rises on the left of a gravel road on the west side of a small creek that spills out from a dam. The trail passes above the dam as it heads uphill towards a marshy valley west of and below the chairlift.

At a spot where the trail drops a little, the upper terminal of the chairlift is visible on a wooded bluff above and to the right; ahead is Brockton Point, beyond which is the First Peak of Mount Seymour proper. The trail now swings to the right, avoiding this peak, then turns back a little on the way to Second and Third peaks. The last part involves a little rock scrambling without any clearly defined trail in places. When snow is on the ground, a short section by Second Peak poses some danger because of the steep drop-off to the left.

For those who go on to the final summit, the extra effort involved is fully repaid by the views in all directions with, as a special feature, the northward continuation of the long ridge on which Mount Seymour stands, Mount Bishop being a prominent feature in the distance. If lunching on the summit, spare a scrap or two for those unlicensed beggars, the whiskey jacks; they will demand a handout anyway. Note, too, that care is necessary on the return, especially in mist or cloud, as it is easy to get into bluffs and gullies east or west of the main ridge.

As an extension for well-equipped and experienced groups only, Mount Elsay, the next rise along the ridge to the north of Third Peak, is a possible destination though it does involve some bushwhacking and, more important, a loss of altitude of some 150 m (500 ft) that has to be regained on the return. To find the markers, go downhill to the west from the final notch before Third Peak, staying about halfway up the righthand side of the gully. The taped trail curves north, dropping to the ridge on the west side of Mount Seymour. Go along this ridge for 200 metres or so, then into the gully to the north. From the bottom of the gully, the track rises steeply northwest past a rocky outcrop; it then crosses a rock slide before levelling off on a north-running ridge. Ascend the peak of Elsay (1420 m/4650 ft) directly from the ridge.

Return may be by the same route, though a loop trip is also possible. For this, descend east from the low point of Mount Elsay's south ridge, work down a rock slide, then go right on the Elsay Lake Trail (Hike 9), the complete hike taking about 9 hours.

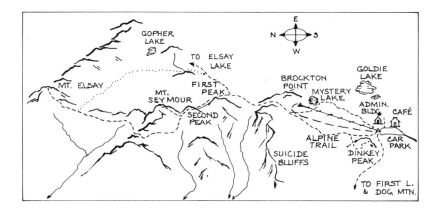

9 ELSAY LAKE

Round trip 18 km (11 mi)
Allow 13 hours
High point 1260 m (4150 ft)
Elevation loss 500 m (1640 ft)
Best July to October
Map Coquitlam 92G/7

Here is a day hike to the midpoint near Gopher Lake, or an overnight backpack for experienced hikers who are prepared to do more ascending on the return than on the way out: a matter of 500 m (1640 ft), no less, from Elsay Lake back to the intersection of this trail with the one to Mount Seymour just before Brockton Point. The beauty of this trip is that you speedily reach quite wild alpine country where you can be alone with the wilderness without travelling far from Vancouver.

At present, the latter part is little more than a marked route, so care is necessary; however, the Provincial Parks branch is upgrading the trail, making its existence worth recording, especially as there is a wilderness cabin at the destination.

From Mount Seymour's upper parking lot, follow the main peak trail past Brockton Point, then turn sharp right at the painted sign announcing that Elsay Lake is 8 km (5 mi) farther. Follow the markers east, then north, going right before passing the park's perimeter sign and beginning to drop. Finally the trail levels off in a rock basin behind and below the main peak of Seymour, with the dome of Runner Peak pointing skyward behind.

Next, after you rise over a subsidiary ridge, you enter a boulder-strewn basin and cross the two streams that drain into Gopher Lake, with the steep

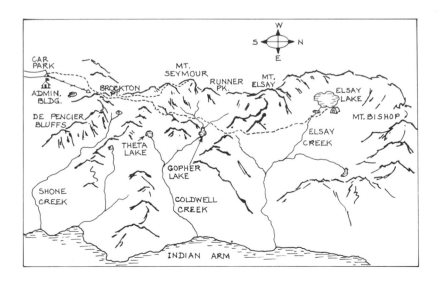

Runner Peak and Mt. Elsay loom over the trail — *W. Cadillac*

slopes of Mount Elsay to the northwest. Beyond here (at the time of writing), the trail is still rough so you may decide that this is far enough, giving you a round trip of about 6 hours.

If you do continue, follow the flagged route over the timbered east ridge of Mount Elsay to enter the valley drained by Elsay Creek. Once in this, you descend to the valley floor with the creek to negotiate before you reach the cabin. There is at present no bridge and the easiest crossing is some distance upstream from where you meet the creek. A route marked with white paint and ribbons leads you up the southwest side, at first away from, then back to the creek. Don't forget to unbuckle the belt of your pack just in case of a slip. Once across, follow the flagged route through the bush, over an open swampy area on its northeast side, past little Elsay Lake, and so to the cabin.

Sagging bridge by Old Buck Trail

NORTH SHORE

10 THREE-CHOP TRAIL

Round trip to Deep Cove Lookout
13 km (7.8 mi)
High point 760 m (2500 ft)
Elevation gain 610 m (2000 ft)
Allow 5 hours
Best May to November

From Deep Cove Lookout to
Brockton Point 8.5 km (5.25 mi)
High point 1260 m (4150 ft)
Elevation gain 450 m (1500 ft)
Allow 4 hours
Best June to October
Map Coquitlam 92G/7

This accommodating trail will give you a satisfying early- or late-season low-level walk, or if you desire more exercise, it will provide access to the alpine slopes of Mount Seymour in conjunction with the provincial park's Perimeter Trail. "Three-chop" itself gets its name from the triple blaze marks once used to identify it; these, though now indistinct, may still be seen on a number of trees as you ascend. One bonus feature: this outing avoids the high-use areas of Mount Seymour Park so that you have relative peace as you wander.

To reach the start, take the left turnoff to Mount Seymour Park from the Parkway, then, just before the park gate, go sharp right on Indian River Road. After 800 m go left on Indian River Crescent and stay with this as it merges with Indian River Road again until, at a right turn, you see facing you a B.C. Hydro access road with a Baden-Powell Trail sign on your left, 3.3 km

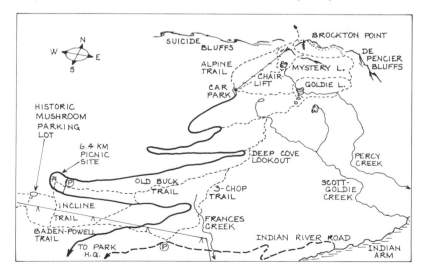

(2 mi) from the park road. Park here, clear of traffic, and follow the rough Hydro road up to the right-of-way. The trail is directly in front of you as you walk underneath the wires towards the forested slope ahead. From here, you ascend steadily in fairly old second-growth forest, crossing a few creeks en route.

After about 90 minutes, you become aware of a trail joining from the left. Thereafter you continue along what you will learn is the Old Buck Trail once you reach its junction with Perimeter Trail a short distance to the right of Deep Cove Lookout—a possible destination if you do not wish to go higher.

To return from the lookout, retrace your steps to the Old Buck Trail and stay with it as it swings gradually westward across the face of the mountain. Next, a short distance above the Park Highway, comes a fork to the right, its destination a picnic site at 6.4 km (4 mi) on the highway. It does not matter which fork you take; both lead to the Baden-Powell Trail, along which you return to your vehicle, but the right fork gives you the longer walk. If you stay with Old Buck, cross the highway, walk 50 metres uphill and follow the B.C. Hydro access road down to the powerline. Then continue to the B-P Trail and turn left when you reach it.

On the other route, you come first to the old road and some picnic tables. Continue westward to where the highway turns back east; just below the bend, on the other side of the thoroughfare, look for the sign pointing out the route to the B-P Trail. Even on Incline Trail, as this is called, you have a choice. You may go straight down the crest of the ridge or you may fork right once more and descend via the site of the Historic Mushroom car park. This was the terminus of a road up the mountain, but it has now acquired a good growth of alder. Continue downward on the west side of the ridge to the B-P Trail, a short distance below the powerline. Go left along it and as you travel note the two trails already mentioned coming in from the left. Finally, cross the Park Highway and follow the Scout Trail back to your vehicle.

If at Deep Cove Lookout you decide to continue north along Perimeter Trail, you eventually reach a junction with a sign pointing left to Goldie Lake. Keep right, dropping slightly at first then rising again till you come to another sign: "To the Ski Lodge." Follow this trail for about 100 metres to a fork. Go right and uphill, following orange markers till finally the bluffy outcrops around Brockton Point appear on your right. To continue, veer westward to avoid bluffs, then go north again roughly following the route of the new chairlift and you will eventually reach Brockton Point—a fair destination, given that you have to descend the mountain. This last section is for experienced hikers only; it involves quite a long day's walking and a considerable gain in vertical height, and the last part is on a trail identified only by diamond-shaped signs.

First peak from meadow east of Brockton Point

HOWE SOUND

11 SUNSET TRAIL

Round trip to Yew Lake 14 km (9 mi)
Allow 5 hours
High point 915 m (3000 ft)
Elevation gain 855 m (2800 ft)
Best May to October

Round trip to Mt. Strachan 22 km
(14 mi)
Allow 9 hours
High point 1454 m (4769 ft)
Elevation gain 1400 m (4600 ft)
Best July to October
Map Vancouver North 92G/6

As an alternative to the road access into Cypress Provincial Park from the south, the trail from Squamish Highway to Yew Lake at its western end should appeal to the hiker who prefers cool forests and the peace of the trail to the noise and smell of internal combustion engines.

To reach the start of this hike, take Highway 99 north along Howe Sound to the Sunset Marina sign about 4.8 km (3 mi) beyond the right fork at Horseshoe Bay. Park on the left just past the marina entrance and cross to the second road (gated) going uphill right. Despite its forbidding sign, this is your approach, the other being a private driveway. Continue up it and look for the start of the trail on the right where the road bends left at a small water tower.

After about 45 minutes you swing south, then continue climbing quite steeply in a general southeasterly direction before turning back to the north-

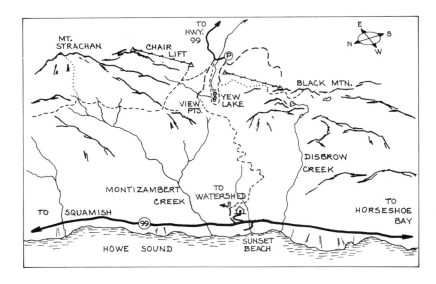

Yew Lake

west. Another hour or less sees the trail emerge from the trees onto the marshy area to the west of Yew Lake, with Mount Strachan rising to the north, Hollyburn to the east, and Black Mountain a little west of south. For the moment, however, head for the belt of trees to the left, skirting the wet areas, and pick up a track to join an old road, a left turn onto which takes you to a viewpoint over Howe Sound and its islands—a possible destination for an easy day.

For a more strenuous alternative, head for the Howe Sound Crest Trail, visible above from the same road (for its beginning walk back a short distance to the right). Follow this trail to the meadow northwest of Mount Strachan. From there, a taped route to the right leads you up a steep gully from which you may reach the dip between the two summits, being careful to follow the tapes to the left part way up to avoid a nasty little overhang. This route should probably not be attempted on snow, but its successful completion when conditions are favourable makes a circuit possible with return by the traditional route (Hike 3) leading you back to Collins Ski Run, Yew Lake and the top of the Sunset Trail.

Along the ridge to The Lions— *W. Cadillac*

HOWE SOUND

12 UNNECESSARY MOUNTAIN

Round trip 9.5 km (6 mi)
Allow 7 hours
High point 1510 m (4950 ft)
Elevation gain 1310 m (4300 ft)
Best July to October
Map Vancouver North 92G/6

This mountain owes its odd name to the fact that at one time local climbers had to make their way up and over it en route to The Lions. Although long superseded as the main approach, the trail to Unnecessary Mountain does provide an alternative, besides offering a hike in its own right.

Driving north from Horseshoe Bay on Highway 99, you turn off sharp right just before the bridge over Harvey Creek in Lions Bay village and shortly thereafter go right again on Oceanview Road. Stay left at its fork with Panorama and continue on it as it winds its sinuous way upward to its termination at a gate just before a water tower where very limited parking space is available. Walk up the road that starts as blacktop but soon reverts to gravel. You gradually swing from south to north, noting, as you pass, the admonition to hikers regarding their behaviour in the village watershed. Then, just before a "No Trespassing" sign, your trail goes off steeply uphill, its beginning marked with orange squares supplemented with a few statistics. So from about 275 m (900 ft) you head upwards into the forest, with the warning that you have 4.7 km (2.9 mi) to go.

Your first excitement comes right at the start with a scramble through a deep ditch, and thereafter come some steep stretches that may need hands, as well as a few that have fallen trees for you to get over. However, the trail does level off from time to time, and as you get higher and the trees thin out you have some striking views of your objective, a seemingly insurmountable cliff from one vantage point. The outlook over Howe Sound, too, is worth your attention if you can spare time from the final steep ascent to look around.In the end, just short of the summit, your ridge joins the one used by the Howe Sound Crest Trail and a left turn soon brings you to the top.

For many, Unnecessary itself will be a sufficient goal, the round trip to that point taking about 7 hours because of the steep trail. For experienced groups who had the foresight to park a second car at the end of the Harvey Creek logging road system, a loop trip is possible, however. From Unnecessary strike north along the ridge towards the West Lion and return to the road by the "new" Lions trail, which leaves the ridge just to the south of that peak (Hike 13). Yet another possibility, also using a two-car shuttle, is to combine this outing with a hike along Howe Sound Crest Trail (Hike 2).

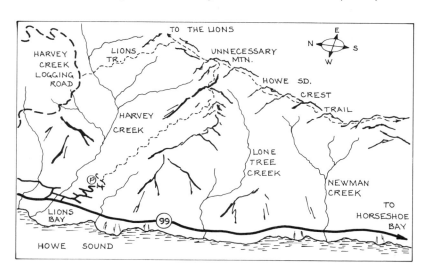

HOWE SOUND

13 LIONS TRAIL

Round trip 15 km (9 mi)
Allow 7 hours
High point 1525 m (5000 ft)
Elevation gain 1280 m (4200 ft)
Best July to October
Map Vancouver North 92G/6

That this trail, one of the most popular in the lower mainland, exists at all is largely the result of efforts by Paul Binkert of the B.C. Mountaineering Club. As you use it, therefore, think gratefully of the voluntary efforts that went into its construction.

The trail gives access to the ridge on which the Lions are situated; you reach it from Highway 99 by turning right for Lions Bay on Oceanview Road, left over Harvey Creek on Cross Creek Road then right on Centre Road. Next go left on Bayview Road for 1.1 km (0.7 mi), turn left again briefly on Mountain Drive, then swing left on Sunset Drive to the gate which bars further progress. Note that parking may be a problem, especially on weekends, so be careful where you leave your vehicle. The old logging road beyond the gate, adorned with an admonition to hikers, is the route. Follow this as it switchbacks upward. After about 45 minutes, take the right fork at a main junction (left leads to Brunswick Mountain). A little later, go right and continue uphill, heading south and east back towards the valley of Harvey Creek; the road becomes a trail in the process as a result of rockfall and wash-outs. Finally, a well-marked trail goes off right, drops into the creek valley, then heads towards the Lions ridge to the south of the West Lion. After crossing Harvey Creek, this trail goes up via a prominent ridge of tall trees, passing a small side summit (a possible camping spot, complete with views but lacking water).

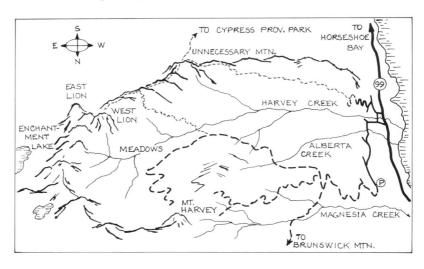

East Lion from the base of the West

From here continue to the main ridge south of the West Lion where the old trail over Unnecessary Mountain (now part of the Howe Sound Crest Trail) joins it from the right. This trail, still incomplete, is intended to head north to Porteau via Deeks Lake (Hike 16). The West Lion itself is a rock climb and, as such, should be attempted only by properly equipped parties with experienced leaders. The same caveat applies to the East Lion which is also out of bounds, being in the Greater Vancouver watershed. The ridge crest is, however, sufficiently spectacular with views over the Capilano valley towards Cathedral Mountain and more distant peaks, and west over Howe Sound and its islands towards the Sechelt Peninsula and Vancouver Island. From the high point before the notch at the base of the West Lion, too, you have a grandstand view of climbers on their ascent to the summit.

HOWE SOUND

14 MOUNT HARVEY

Round trip 12.5 km (7.8 mi)
Allow 7 hours
High point 1705 m (5590 ft)
Elevation gain 1465 m (4800 ft)
Best July to October
Map Vancouver North 92G/6

For long enough the ridge and peak that make up this beautifully shaped mountain were accessible only by a bushwhack from a spur that branches left off the Harvey Creek logging road a short distance after it has parted from the Brunswick Mountain approach. All that changed when Halvor Lunden created a route to the ridge whereby you stay with the West Lion approach until just before the road is blocked by a slide. Here on the right is a tree signposted "Mt. Harvey"; across the road up a steep bank on the left is the first orange marker.

After scrambling up the bank, you make your way up the side of a gully, on the opposite side of which cascades a small waterfall. Soon the trail starts to turn away from the creek, entering a section of young forest briefly before swinging back into the tall timber. This process is repeated as you continue to zigzag steeply upward then skirt the head of a wide basin and strike east to attain the main ridge. This happens at a burned-over area offering a spectacular view of the neighbouring West Lion. The trail now follows the ridge, beautiful in season with various heaths, flowers, small bushes and trees until, after one more stretch of silver forest, a final scramble brings you out on the rocky summit.

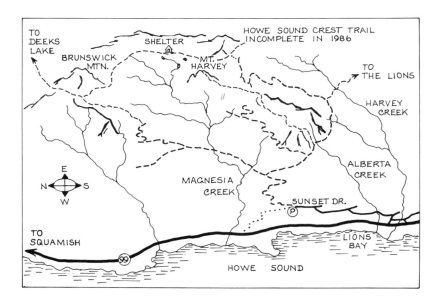

Mist in the forest

From here, the views to the west across Howe Sound match the best, while naturally the Lions, somewhat diminished from your lofty eyrie, fill up the picture to the southeast. From here, also, in addition to more distant views, you may see to your left front the northward extension of the Howe Sound Crest Trail swinging across from Mount Harvey's eastern ridge to meadows around the head of Magnesia Creek and the shelter hut located there.

For strong, experienced hikers an alternative return is by the eastern ridge to meet the Crest Trail, going right on it, then dropping to the upper end of the logging road up Harvey Creek. On this you eventually link up with the Lions Trail and your original route. By so doing, however, you add the best part of 6 km (3.5 mi) to your trip, a possible deterrent.

And the name? According to J. T. Walbran's **British Columbia Coast Names,** like so many other coastal features, it commemorates an eighteenth-century British naval officer, one who served under Admiral Howe. Now the subordinate looks down peacefully upon his one-time commander.

Spring scene on Mount Brunswick— *H. Lunden*

HOWE SOUND

15 BRUNSWICK MOUNTAIN

Round trip 15 km (9 mi)
Allow 8 hours
High point 1785 m (5855 ft)
Elevation gain 1550 m (5100 ft)
Best July to October
Map Vancouver North 92G/6

This prominent ridge and peak, immediately to the north of Mount Harvey (HMS **Brunswick** was the ship Harvey commanded) has the same vehicle approach as the previous two hikes. Likewise the first 40-minute portion of the trail is identical with the Harvey Creek approach until you go left at the first fork, while the Harvey Creek Trail swings back south.

After the parting of the ways, you cross Magnesia Creek. Then comes another fork and you go steeply uphill to the right, switchbacking up the deteriorating logging road to where it ends just below the standing timber at 1052 m (3450 ft). From here the Brunswick Trail goes steeply up the fall line to a spur, at which point it heads back east towards the gully that gives access to the summit ridge. A degree of caution is necessary on this last stretch, which is steep and may be tricky, especially in snow. The short summit ridge itself is narrow, but all-round views from the peak are more than adequate compensation for the expenditure of energy involved in getting there, the mountain vistas north and east being particularly striking.

On the steep part of the ascent, at a little over 1525 m (5000 ft) the Howe Sound Crest Trail intersects your route on its passage from Deeks Lake to Magnesia Meadows. And mention of this north-south connector suggests an option for you if you are finding Brunswick just a little daunting. Hat Mountain (the rationale for its name is obvious if you look up at it from the highway) lies west of the point where the Crest Trail crosses the saddle. From there, head west for about 1 km (0.6 m) to its brim and crown. Although there is no trail, the ridge is open and route-finding is easy.

If, however, you have attained the peak and feel like turning your hike into a loop trip, you may head south on the Howe Sound Crest Trail when you get back down to it. Follow the trail via Magnesia Meadows over the pass to the east of Mount Harvey and drop down to the old Harvey Creek logging road for your return, the distance back to your original junction being approximately 5.7 km (3 mi) longer than the direct route.

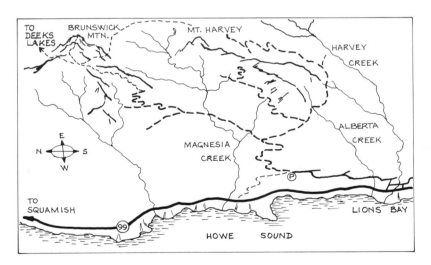

HOWE SOUND

16 DEEKS LAKES

Round trip 20 km (12.4 mi)
Allow 10 hours
High point 1220 m (4000 ft)
Elevation gain 1190 m (3900 ft)
Best late June to October
Map Squamish 92G/11

This hike, over part of the as yet uncompleted Howe Sound Crest Trail, makes a pleasant day's outing, but it may also form part of a crossover to Lions Bay for two-car parties, a shorter trip (though with more climbing) than the return to the original starting point near Porteau. To reach this, drive north on Highway 99 for a little over 10 km (6 mi) beyond Lions Bay village to a clearly marked parking area. The trail begins almost opposite, designated by a trailhead sign and orange markers.

Of the three lakes in the valley, only the lowest has been officially named and it has existed in its present state for little more than 90 years, having been enlarged by damming to provide water for a gravel-extracting operation; nowadays it exists as a popular camping and fishing spot in its own right. The trail to it has been upgraded as well, replacing an approach via the creek that was judged to be too steep.

On your trip, you first pass a powerline, then join an old logging road on which you go right. Despite minor turnoffs, the main track is clear as you gradually turn into the valley of the creek. After about 40 minutes you pass the older creek trail on your right, then shortly beyond a small pond, your marked trail swings to the left, rising steeply from the old road to avoid a severe slide area and heading over the bluffs in old forest before descend-

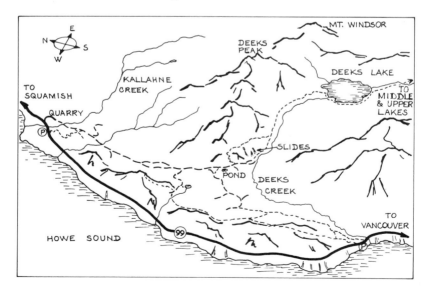

Looking up Deeks Lake towards Mount Brunswick— *D. Ellis*

ing to meet it once more. Soon, entering a recently created provincial park, you come within earshot of the creek again with Phi Alpha Falls on your right as you switchback up before emerging from the forest a little above the first lake.

Turn right here along the lakeshore. Cross the outflow on chained logs and follow the improved trail around the lake's south side before the valley closes in again as you ascend, first on the west and then the east side of the creek, to the middle lake, its waters turquoise in sunshine. As you make your way along the lake, you are conscious of the horns of Brunswick Mountain ahead and Hat Mountain's truncated cone to your right. Beyond the lake your rewards are the sight of a fine waterfall and finally the irregularly shaped upper lake with its protruding appendix to the west, which you cross on rocks if you wish to proceed.

This is a beautiful setting for a camping spot if you are backpacking. Should you wish to continue to Lions Bay, however, you must follow the trail up out of the valley to the col north of Brunswick Mountain. Once you have intersected the trail to that mountain (Hike 15), you descend steadily on it to reach Lions Bay after a trip of roughly 19 km (11.8 mi) with a high point of about 1525 m (5000 ft).

Note: The upper lake is now popularly known as Brunswick Lake.

HOWE SOUND

17 DEEKS PEAK

Round trip 17.5 km (10.8 mi)
Allow 8 hours
High point 1674 m (5490 ft)
Elevation gain 1616 m (5300 ft)
Best July to October
Map Squamish 92G/11

While young tigers may make straight for the peak from the Deeks Lake Trail, a little less rigorous route does exist, one that will get you at least as far as the small unnamed lake at the head of the west branch of Kallahne Creek, the drainage for the mountain's northwest slopes. This trail, moreover, has the advantage of providing en route some views across Howe Sound to the Mount Sedgwick massif and to the peaks of the Tantalus farther north.

For your start, you use the same parking lot as for Deeks Lake, and you set out on the same trail, but only for the first twenty minutes or so. After crossing the highway, follow the trail to join the old logging road as for Deeks Lake, but this time, in about 5 minutes, watch for and go left on a washed out and somewhat overgrown old road. From now on the two trails diverge as you turn back slightly north, gaining height by way of a number of long switchbacks, in the course of which you approach the creek then swing away from it again.

Next comes another overgrown stretch of road, followed by a crossing of the west fork of the creek, which may pose problems at times of high water,

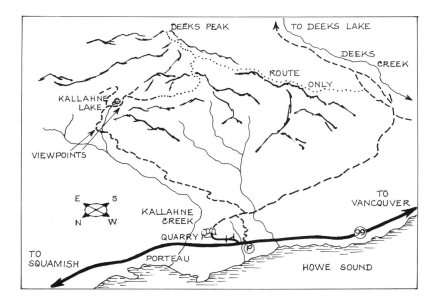

View up Howe Sound from the powerline

though late in the year the water may all have gone underground. Beyond the creek pick your way across a rockfall, find the deteriorating road again and turn back on it up the creek to the lake. Here, at something like 1070 m (3500 ft), with a comfortable viewpoint you may feel that you have had enough exercise, a one-way hike of about 4.5 km (3.0 mi) behind you.

If you wish to continue, make your way over the log jam which bridges the outlet and head south along the west side of the lake, working up the right branch of the now very eroded old road to its end at the edge of the standing timber. From here on there is no perceptible trail, only a taped route starting to the right of a draw full of logs and other debris. After travelling roughly southward in an ascending traverse, you swing east and scramble up steeply, eventually reaching the main ridge on which you turn southward again towards the summit. This you will arrive at in about another hour, it being necessary on the way to surmount a subsidiary summit, itself almost as high as the main peak. Once there, however, you may enjoy the fruits of your labours, the outstanding views west across Howe Sound and its islands, north to the mountains of Garibaldi Park and around by Sky Pilot to the mountains of the southeast.

The final part of this hike is obviously not for beginners, consisting as it does merely of a taped route. It is fairly lengthy into the bargain, and snow lies until late in the year on the high country. These considerations aside, it is well worth the attention of experienced groups.

18 MOUNT CAPILANO

Round trip 26 km (16 mi)
Allow 10 hours
High point 1686 m (5529 ft)
Elevation gain 1600 m (5250 ft)
Best July to October
Map Squamish 92G/11

This mountain is only for the truly fit; in fact, if the gate at the end of Furry Creek logging road is locked, you might consider the mountain's ascent as an overnight backpack, stopping at Beth Lake—a picturesque spot, though its surroundings do have some mosquitoes. To reach the start, drive north on the Squamish Highway just over 27 km (17 mi) north of Horseshoe Bay turnoff until, about halfway up a steepish hill, the approach road goes off sharp right, with a little parking space before the gate.

Stay right at the first junction and cross Furry Creek, then its tributary, Phyllis Creek, which you follow to the next fork at a point where the B.C. Hydro lines are almost directly overhead. Go left here, recross Phyllis Creek, and head back towards the south side of Furry Creek valley, rising as you go. Next, after some 7 km (4.4 mi), shortly after the crossing of Beth Creek, your taped route (actually an ancient logging road) goes uphill to the right. You now rise steadily, keeping the creek on your right and heading for trees above the logged area. Finally, at 1050 m (3500 ft), you reach the lake, its high rock ramparts behind it.

The trail to Capilano goes right, crosses the outlet on the log jam, swings a little north, then doubles back to ascend the ridge west of the lake. At first you are in trees, but then you emerge into a rock basin with the upper ridge beyond. Cross this and head up to the higher country, travelling mainly south. From here a short hike brings you out on subalpine surroundings with one lower ridge stretching south, pointing across the upper Capilano River to Brunswick Mountain and the Lions; the peak itself, lying half left, involves a little scrambling.

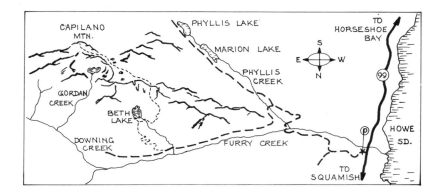

Ramparts above Beth Lake

The open summit has a panoramic view, well worth the effort even if you have had to start at the highway. To the north, you can see Sky Pilot and beyond it the mountains of Garibaldi Park; to the east, other giants of the southern Coast Range; westward, across Howe Sound, you have the southern Tantalus peaks, and to the south, you get a different perspective on Vancouver's local summits—from the backside.

Note that had you stayed right at the powerline fork, you would have had a gentle low-level walk to Marion and Phyllis lakes, the latter located some 8 km (5 mi) from the highway at the boundary of the Capilano watershed on the borders of Chief Capilano's domain, for despite its Italianate appearance, the name, according to the Akriggs' **British Columbia Place Names,** is actually an anglicized version of the hereditary title for the chief of the North Vancouver Indian Band.

HOWE SOUND

19 PETGILL LAKE

Round trip 9.5 km (6 mi)
Allow 5 hours
High point 795 m (2600 ft)
Elevation gain 640 m (2100 ft)
Best March to November
Map Squamish 92G/11

Although it makes a popular hike for a warm day because it winds through shady woods, the trail to the lake is also suited for winter walking since its high point is little more than 790 m (2600 ft) above sea level. You start about 4.8 km (3 mi) north of Britannia Beach, after parking at Murrin Park just beyond Browning Lake at the top of a long hill.

The signposted trail begins on the east side of the highway about 350 metres north of the parking area. At first it climbs steeply via the bluffs overlooking the road, but soon you are in forest. Despite the tree cover there are nicely spaced viewpoints, the first of which comes at a point looking more or less west across Howe Sound to the mountains beyond. The second, shortly after, faces north and gives views of Stawamus Chief and, at a greater distance, Mount Garibaldi and the Black Tusk.

Next the trail climbs a little more before dropping slightly to join an old logging road with which you stay as it heads east then south. The road becomes completely overgrown at the point where the trail turns off left. From here, you make your way over several lateral ridges, the first providing a distant view to the southwest. Finally, after descending into yet another dark gully, you come to a sign and pointer for Goat Ridge, and about 50 metres beyond, some 100 metres before the lake, a trail marked with tapes goes off to the right. The lake itself lies among trees in a pleasant basin with the western end of Goat Ridge rising above it to the east.

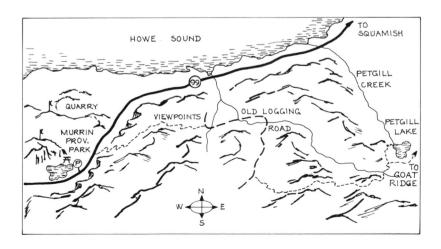

West over Petgill Lake

The trail to the ridge, already mentioned, gives you a much more strenuous hike though a rewarding one, despite adding another 975 m (3200 ft) of climbing on a route that is sketchy here and there. First it heads northwest, then swings east and starts switchbacking relentlessly upward until it reaches the end of the main ridge at 1433 m (4700 ft), after which you begin to have views in all directions as the trees become interspersed with attractive meadows. Finally, at the high point—1769 m (5800 ft)—comes a close-up view of Sky Pilot, while Garibaldi and Mamquam fill in the scene to the north and northeast. However, such an extension adds at least three hours to your trip, so it should be saved for the long days of summer.

20 STAWAMUS CHIEF

Round trip to
First Peak 6.4 km (4 mi)
Second Peak 9.5 km (6 mi)
Third Peak 11 km (7 mi)
Allow up to 4 hours for Third Peak
High point 650 m (2138 ft)
Elevation gain 610 m (2000 ft)
Best March to November
Map Squamish 92G/11

Everyone knows Stawamus Chief, the great rock mass that towers over the highway just south of Squamish townsite. Rock climbers scale its face by various routes, but the ordinary walker can achieve any one of the three peaks, or all three if he likes, if he keeps to the rear of the rock. Once the climbing is past, he can enjoy the summit view of Mount Garibaldi and the Tantalus Range—and suffer the industrial pollution of Woodfibre Mill, which causes an almost permanent pall of smoke over that part of Howe Sound.

To reach the parking spot, turn right off Highway 99 at the Chief viewpoint 1.2 km (0.7 mi) north of Shannon Falls, cross the lot and turn right along an old road. Keep left thereafter until it ends about 700 metres along at a one-time quarry just south of the Chief. The trail starts up the rocks at the east end, ascending for the first 50 m (175 ft) or so on a flight of wooden steps, near the top of which a new trail enters from the right having crossed the turbulent Olesen Creek on a bridge completed in September 1986. This trail, which begins at Shannon Falls Park, offers an attractive alternative beginning to the hike, adding only 30 or 40 minutes to the day.

Ignore a trail to the right that recrosses the creek en route to the top of the falls, then, for First Peak, go left at the next junction a few metres on. This

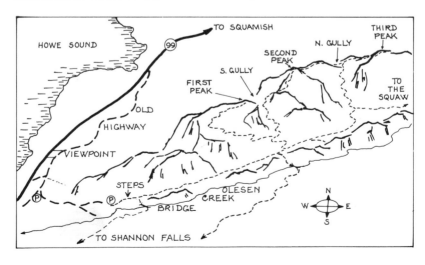

Looking south over First Peak— *P. Durnford*

leads in a number of switchbacks to a bluff, then goes south over a shoulder and on open rock to the objective. Second Peak is reached by staying on the trail to First Peak as far as the second fork. Turn right here and continue up a gully, then follow a rocky ledge into the open. Turn right again into a rock cleft crossed by a rather hair-raising log bridge, then head steeply up to the rocky slopes of the crest ridge. Walk north along this to the summit.

To reach Third Peak, which is the highest, continue along the crest, descending into the saddle between Second and Third. This saddle, the upper terminal of the North Gully, is followed by a junction with an alternative trail to Third Peak that avoids Second Peak. Continue into the wooded trench and along a rockface from which the open is reached by a ledge. From here turn first left, then right, and walk on open rock to the summit.

The alternative trail, bypassing Second Peak, is reached by leaving the First Peak trail at the second fork and staying right, walking through tall trees to a logging road and picking up the route again in second growth. Go left at the junction with the Squaw trail and ascend a gully, at the crest of which you meet the trail from the second summit.

Mamquam Mountain from the Squaw

HOWE SOUND

21 STAWAMUS SQUAW

Round trip 14.5 km (9 mi)
Allow 5 hours
High point 610 m (2000 ft)
Elevation gain 550 m (1800 ft)
Best March to November
Map Squamish 92G/11

This summit remains modestly in the background while the Chief lords it over the Squamish valley; still, the lady has a beauty all her own and the route has ample variety. Vehicle approach and the first part of the trail are the same as for the Chief, staying right at the marked forks, the third of which is about 45 minutes after setting out.

The trail stays just below the bluffs behind Third Peak, and care has to be taken at a couple of spots: first where a small slide has left the slanting rock bare and slippery when wet or icy, and second where the trail drops steeply to the right to bring you down to the floor of the upper valley with its small ponds. Turn north (left) here and climb gently, following an old overgrown road, one from which views begin to open out to the south where the precipitous mass of the Chief's Third Peak fills the eye. The route eventually brings you onto an old logging road. Follow this left for a short distance to where markers take you uphill left into the forest and on to your objective with its demolished Forest Service lookout.

From here Garibaldi and Mamquam dominate the northern horizon, and southeast, the finger of Mount Habrich points heavenward. Across Howe Sound, Mount Sedgwick rears above Woodfibre, and north of that are the proud peaks of the Tantalus range. Only a dullard could remain uninspired by such beauty.

The return route may be the same, but if you can arrange a second car you may plan a crossover whereby you descend by the Stawamus River, reducing your return time by half. To do this, drive on north a little until just past the bridge over the Stawamus River. Turn right and proceed eastward through Valleycliffe. Once beyond the subdivision, turn right to join the MacMillan-Bloedel logging road up the valley. The first fork on the right after the junction is the one you take, notwithstanding the Watershed sign. From here drive along the east bank of the river to park in a wide area just before a bridge. Thus having made the necessary preparations beforehand, when you leave the summit you follow the trail back down to the logging road and then keep going left at the next three junctions. You will eventually arrive at your car.

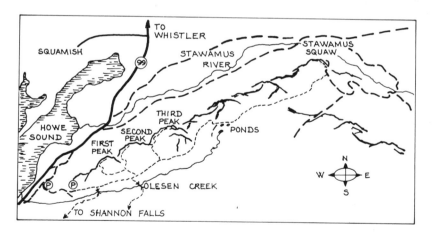

22 MOUNT RODERICK

Round trip 20.5 km (12.7 mi)
Allow 10 hours or overnight
High point 1475 m (4840 ft)
Best June to October
Map Squamish 92G/11

Since Western Forest Products, owners of Woodfibre Mill, do not allow private vehicles to use their road, your hike now starts from sea level, and for that reason you may consider making a backpack trip into such a magnificent and lonely alpine area as this, with one of the lakes en route, Henrietta or Sylvia, as alternative destinations for a day trip. Whatever your intentions, you must first cross Howe Sound by ferry from Darrell Bay, its terminal parking lying to the left of Highway 99 a short distance south of Shannon Falls Provincial Park as you travel towards Squamish from Vancouver. It is a good plan also to check that the area is open for hiking before you embark and to have an alternative destination in mind in case access is denied.

Once across the sound and resigned to the smell of the pulp mill, make for the First Aid Building to register. When you leave, you may follow the road as it swings uphill towards the dormitories or you may ascend a flight of steps which cuts off the first bend. Stay with the travelled road as it turns first towards Mill Creek then swings back to the south. In the area cleared for B.C. Hydro powerlines, you keep right at all junctions, then follow the road into forest as it rises parallel with and on the north side of Woodfibre Creek. Finally, after about 6 km (3.7 mi), the road ends at a creek in a deep gorge spanned by a smart metal footbridge.

A short distance beyond, the logging road dwindles to a trail that zigzags

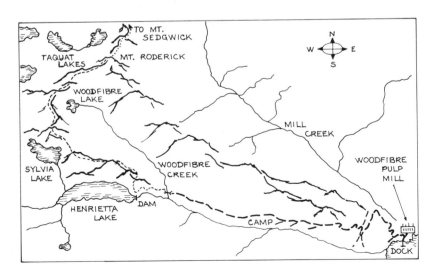

Taquat Lakes from the ridge – *W. Cadillac*

up the ridge, crossing and recrossing the route of the old construction railway to the lake outlet, on the right-hand side of which, near a cabin, a trail goes north up the wooded spur of the ridge. It finally levels off, more or less, at a little over 1220 m (4000 ft). A shallow basin just west of the ridge contains Sylvia Lake, an attractive spot for an overnight camp; Sechelt Ridge stretches southwest from the opposite side of the lake outlet.

The trail to Mount Roderick continues along the ridge, mainly on the north side of the crest, with a sufficient number of ups and downs to try the mettle of the hiker heading for the objective, 1½ hours beyond Sylvia Lake. From Roderick itself, the mass of Mount Sedgwick looms ahead, with the ridge first dropping into a saddle then rising up to its snowfields and rock. This, however, is for experienced parties only, preferably those who can give at least two days to the trip. The country is all beautifully open, with views of the Tantalus Range to the north, Mount Garibaldi to the northeast, and Sky Pilot to the east, giving a sense of grandeur to the occasion. Below are valleys, many of them with lakes and all looking remote and unspoiled.

One final note: Don't forget to sign out on your return to Woodfibre.

From the viewpoint on Mat Hill Trail

SECHELT AND ISLANDS

23 MOUNT GARDNER

Round trip (to peak) 17.5 km (11 mi)
Allow 7 hours
High point 727 m (2383 ft)

Round trip (circuit) 23.5 km (14.5 mi)
Allow 8 hours
High point 660 m (2160 ft)
Good most of the year
Map Vancouver North 92G/6

The Mount Gardner mini-massif on Bowen Island now offers not one but two outings: to the summit(s) of the little mountain or a circuit of its lower slopes with, for reward, unsurpassed views of Howe Sound, as well as, here and there, signs of bygone mining activity. Nor is access from Horseshoe Bay difficult (though you should check ferry times with care). Your day, then, begins on a nautical note, appropriately enough given that both the island and the mountain commemorate long-gone British naval officers. On arrival at Snug Cove, you may go by road via Government and Trunk to your jumping-off point, but the newly created Crippen Regional Park provides a sylvan approach for much of the way.

For this alternative, go right on Cardena about 100 metres from the dock, then turn left at pole 100 (the island's utility poles are numbered, providing handy reference points). From here, continue inland, following a stream on your right until you come to Millars Landing Road. On it you go right to cross the stream, then go left on Farm Road, now a park trail. Stay on this until, just south of Killarney Lake, you emerge on McGee Road where you go left again. Beyond the lake, travel right on Trunk Road for about 800 metres to where a steep service road goes off left between poles 490 and 491.

First you ascend the road until, just past the gate, you see Skid Trail with its orange markers on your left. This trail you follow to the point where it re-emerges on the road, on which you head uphill around a bend before coming on Mat Hill Trail to your right, doubling as part of the circuit trail and as an approach to the peak. Along this you head for your first viewpoint, a handy resting spot for contemplating the peaks along the east shore of Howe Sound. Next comes a junction, with its left fork pointing to Mount Gardner and the right indicating Bowen Bay. Since the Circuit Trail is more rewarding if walked in a clockwise direction, left it is, and after a stiff little pull uphill, you find yourself descending to the road again. In fact, you might have stayed with the road in the first place, though by so doing you would have deprived yourself of the viewpoint.

In any event, turn back uphill on the road to where the peak trail goes off left in a westerly direction, the road itself terminating at a microwave tower a

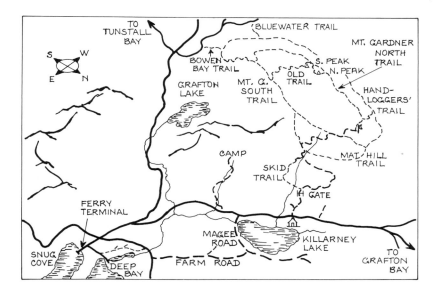

little farther on. Along the way, when the trail turns south, it is joined by a rough path from the right, this one, from Handloggers' Draw on the circuit route, being yet another approach. Soon thereafter you emerge briefly on a rocky bluff with a splendid view westward before returning to the forest for the last lap to the top. Finally, just below the crest, a rather obscure trail forks left. This is the old trail, shorter and steeper than the newer which continues to a T-junction with a sign indicating left for the north summit, a cleared area with a communication installation and a helipad.

The summit you are on is the one for views, those to the west and northwest being especially striking. By contrast, the south summit though a little higher is virtually viewless, but if you wish to visit it after your return to the fork, you must watch for a taped route going sharp left up the side of the rocks about 5 minutes south on the Bowen Bay/Killarney Lake Trail. Continuing south, you descend through forest to yet another fork where you should go left on the Killarney Lake Trail unless you want to return the long way round on the circuit route (don't forget the ferry!).

By going left, you turn northeast on the homeward stretch, through trees at first but later along the lower edge of the great scar, visible from Point Grey, which represents a rocky face on which vegetation has not re-established itself. Before this, however, you have passed on your left the original eastern access route to Mount Gardner's south summit. From now on, keep an eye open for the marked trail going right from the old logging road that you are now on. The last stretch of this trail brings you to a road that you may now begin to recognize as your friendly approach, a little higher than, and round the bend above Mat Hill Trail. All that remains for you is return to Snug Cove and your ferry.

For the complete circuit walk, take the trail just described but go in the opposite direction; that is, go off left from the road on the bend above Mat Hill turnoff. At the important Bowen Bay/Mount Gardner North junction on the southwest of the mountain, stay left, even though you lose 460 m (1500 ft) to a low point on Bowen Hill, at which point a spur trail drops off left to Bowen Bay Road. Here is where you change gear for the steady rise to the stretch called Handloggers' Trail, following yet one more junction with a trail coming from Bluewater subdivision with, a little beyond, the few remaining relics of the one-time Bonanza Mine.

Climbing steadily, you come to the most scenic part of your trip with the slope, open to the north, permitting uninterrupted viewing, even Black Tusk in Garibaldi Park being visible on a clear day, and, of course, the islands of the sound spread out before your eyes. Before leaving this stretch, you may note the steep trail ascending on your right. It is the lower end of the track, the top of which you pass on the trail to the summit.

Going on, you eventually find yourself at Mat Hill junction and from there the road is not far off. But you are still 3.2 km (2 mi) from the ferry, and the end of your day may involve a hectic dash on legs that seem to have become unaccountably heavy since morning.

A rare sighting — *D. Ellis*

Indian pipe— *W. Cadillac*

24 MOUNT ARTABAN

Round trip 10 km (6.2 mi)
Allow 5 hours
High point 610 m (2000 ft)
Good most of the year
Map Vancouver North 92G/6

This one is for the boat owner/hiker, for those with boat-owning friends or for those prepared to charter a water taxi from Horseshoe Bay or Sunset Marina (see Yellow Pages) for the round trip to the east side of Gambier Island. The wharf at Camp Fircom (United Church of Canada) serves as landing stage.

On landing, follow the road towards the caretaker's house. The caretaker is obliging and will point out the start of the trail, which leads west from behind his home. Next pass a road on the left leading to Gambier Estates. Beyond it you come to the trail itself and turn left off the road, which has here swung back right.

A short distance up this trail, a side trail on the right leads north to a saddle and rock knoll with a wooden cross on it. From here there is a good view up Howe Sound and across to the mountains on its east side. The main trail to the demolished Forest Service lookout tower keeps to the left at the intersection. It first heads west, then north once it has reached the west side of the ridge. Thus it continues until it turns east to climb the final stretch to the summit, more or less following the line of the ridge. From it the islands and peaks of Howe Sound are laid out before you. It's a fine spot to while away an hour or so before you return to a life on the ocean wave.

Camp Fircom with Mt. Artaban behind

The island bears the name of the inevitable British naval officer; interestingly enough, however, your little mountain, according to J. T. Walbran's **British Columbia Coast Names,** commemorates a character from fiction, the Fourth Magus who sought Christ but was consistently turned aside from his quest by the needs of his fellow humans.

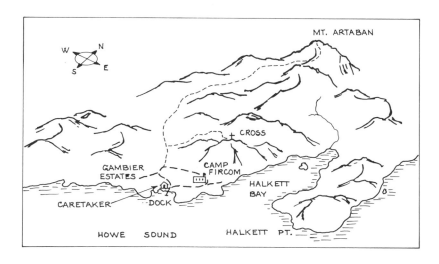

SECHELT AND ISLANDS

25 GAMBIER ISLAND WEST

Round trip (Gambier Lake)
15 km (9.5 mi)
Allow 6 hours
High point 475 m (1550 ft)
Good most of the year
Maps Vancouver North 92G/6,
Squamish 92G/11

If you like to combine your hiking with sailing, the outings available from New Brighton on the southwest coast of Gambier Island should certainly satisfy you, involving as they do not one but two ferry trips from Horseshoe Bay to Langdale and thence to the island. This does require the checking of timetables and noting differences between the weekday and the Sunday schedules—especially for the return connections—but it should not deter you from voyaging aboard the good ship **Dogwood Princess II** once you have crossed Howe Sound.

At New Brighton, walk some 100 metres from the end of the pier, then go left at the fork where the residents' mail boxes are located. On this dirt road you pass "The Farm" then, rather incongruously in this rustic setting, a car graveyard. Next comes a fork with a very old road going off left, but you continue straight ahead until, about 50 minutes from the start, you come to a fork where you do go left, following tapes. The old corduroy road, now little more than a trail, crosses Mannion Creek on the remains of a bridge, after which it is very wet in places for a short time. Here the huge stumps give some idea of the dimensions of the original trees, while the maturing

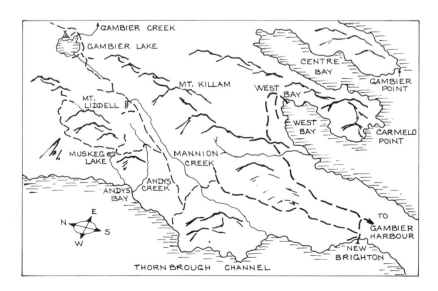

Gambier Lake from the north side

second-growth forest has its appeal as well, showing as it does the regenerative power of nature.

At the next fork, signs inform you that going right will take you to The Lakes in one to two hours, while staying left will lead you down to Andys Bay. Thereafter you wander along uneventfully, rising gently until you are faced with another decision. Left will get you to Third Lake (unofficially named Muskeg Lake) and to Mount Liddell; straight ahead is Gambier Lake itself, presumably the First, or Second, Lake of the cryptic sign.

Staying right, you now rise steadily towards the north-south divide, passing a reed-encircled pool with cottongrass and lilies a little before the highest point. From it you descend some 100 m (330 ft) to your objective, treeringed and with the signs of old campsites indicating its popularity as the destination for an overnight trip. You may, however, easily enjoy an hour by its waters before making a leisurely return to the ferry in time for its early evening sailing.

The hike to the high point along the ridge to the west of you, Mount Liddell, though only some 950 m (3100 ft), will take about 7 hours and may involve an overnight trip, depending on ferry times. If you wish to try it, take the left fork at the junction already mentioned, pass the lake (a possible camping spot), then carry on north along the west side of the mountain following tapes, bypassing the peak on the deteriorating old road, then working back south towards it on a rudimentary route. The summit has fine views across to Rainy River and its mountains on the west, as well as of the islands and the arm of the sea that is Howe Sound: a fitting climax to your brief experience of hiking on Gambier Island.

Mount Steele from trail's end

SECHELT AND ISLANDS

26 LESSER MOUNT STEELE

Round trip (direct) 14 km (8.7 mi)
Allow 6.5 hours

Round trip (including lakes circuit)
18 km (11 mi)
Allow 8 hours
High point 1480 m (4850 ft)
Elevation gain 535 m (1750 ft)
Best June to October
Map Sechelt Inlet 92G/12

Here's a trip that boasts a mountain ascent as well as a circuit of no fewer than five attractive lakes in the high country north of Sechelt village. That being so, your first reference point is the four-way stop on Highway 101 in the village. Here you turn north on Wharf Road, then right on Porpoise Bay Road, passing the Provincial Park, then crossing Gray Creek Bridge nearly 5 km (3.1 mi) beyond.

Now you are faced with a logging company's notice spelling out the usual rules: roads closed to the public apart from evenings, weekends, and holidays. Travelling on, you go right on Upland Road, right again on Carmel Place, at the end of which a small jog takes you onto the logging road. Thus embarked, you go left at the first fork, remaining on West Road (note the sign for Mt. Richardson). Next you stay right at two successive forks, the second by a powerline right-of-way with a sign for Gray Creek (left is for Mt.

Richardson). Now you are directed by arrows, first left then right as you cross the creek and start rising on the south side of its valley. Finally, 21 km (13 mi) from the Sechelt light, you go left at the sign directing you to parking.

Here you may feel that you have been brought to this spot under false pretences, so extensive has been the logging. But one area remains untouched, and it is here that you begin your walk, heading for the tree screen and the trail around the lakes. Very soon the trail forks, left to Gilbert Lake, right to Tannis. For Mount Steele you stay left and proceed, via a succession of trees, ponds and mossy meadows, somewhat damp in places, to Gilbert Lake, where you follow the sign for Edwards Lake. There, at the sign for Mount Steele, go left along the west side of the lake, your route (marked with blue tape) taking you at first through pretty meadows before its steep ascent around the eastern flank of your objective, Lesser Mount Steele. Finally, at a sign to that effect, the taped trail ends at a spot just above the pass between the lesser and greater peaks. At this point, however, trees are sparse and the remaining 61 m (200 ft) over the open, heathery slopes to the summit plateau are easily negotiated, the reward being the views of mountain and water spread before you.

For a more ambitious day, the experienced hiker might contemplate ascending Mount Steele proper by bushwhacking down to the pass from the sign and up the wide open ridge to the peak, thus adding another 90 minutes or so to the day. Whichever you choose, do be careful to return to the same "End of Trail" sign for your descent to the junction at Edwards Lake. Here you may elect to return directly by Gilbert Lake or by the remaining longer leg of the lakes circuit which will lead you over various minor viewpoints and past another three lakes, each with its own beauty, before you finish.

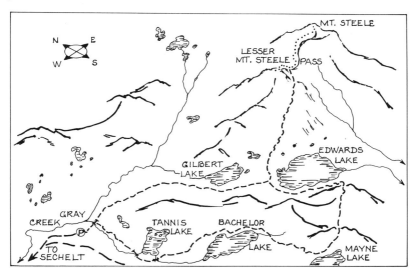

Active Pass and B.C. ferries from the bluffs

SECHELT AND ISLANDS

27 GALIANO ISLAND

Round trip 17 km (10 mi)
Allow 7 hours
High point 335 m (1090 ft)
Good all year
Map Galiano Island 92B/14

One advantage to hikers on this friendly island is that (ferry schedules permitting) you may enjoy its attractions more in the off-season when its roads are quiet than during the summer. In fact, given that the highest point is just over 330 m (1090 ft), it may be on your agenda at any time of the year when you wish to combine a little seafaring with walking.

From Tsawwassen, the Gulf Islands ferry takes you to Sturdies Bay, where you walk a short distance inland before turning left onto Burrill Road. Having passed the pretty little Anglican church, St. Margaret of Scotland, you turn right on Shopland Road, a giant arbutus tree to your left. Now you rise gently for about 20 minutes on what a small plaque calls Hummingbird Hill, passing one or two openings on your left, before going left on a broad track, its beginning marked by a tree root perched on a few stones.

Your track becomes a road with houses (Warbler Road) as you go forward to meet Bluff Drive which, despite its grandiose title, is little more than a country lane. On it go right, but at the Bluff Park sign turn left for an outstanding view of Active Pass, one that is repeated as you walk to the right along the clifftop. With the approach of Georgeson Bay, you are forced inland by the steep slope on your left hand, but where you meet Bluff Drive again you go left immediately on a foot-trail. At the foot of the slope, be careful to go right to reach the road (the trail straight ahead takes you down to a little bay with no exit). Descend this road (Highland Drive) to the left to Georgeson Bay Road, where you go left again then right on Active Pass Road to round the head of the bay, finally going off right on a disused MacMillan-Bloedel forest road. This rises gradually as you travel west, giving another series of fine marine and island views, the one back to Mayne Island being particularly striking. Now you should be keeping an eye out for a mossy old road on the right, its entrance marked with orange and red tapes, for this will be your route up Mount Galiano. Although steep here and there, the route poses no difficulty if you stay with the tapes as it goes west around a rocky bluff then swings back right on meadow before coming out on an old road. Go right here a little, then take the track through the salal for a quick route to the summit ridge (for another viewpoint, you should continue on the road a little further, then fork right).

You may return by the same route, but you may also follow the old road downhill by going left after leaving the top, right at a fork with another old logging road, left on Lord Road, and right on Morgan Road to arrive at Georgeson Bay Road at a point where the highway splits to accommodate a large maple. Go right here and then left on Bluff Drive, which will take you uphill back to the park overlooking Active Pass. If, however, you feel venturesome, go left before that on the track that promises No Exit plus a number of other negatives. After a short time, go right at a T-junction and follow this trail through the forest, stepping daintily here and there to avoid evidence of horse traffic, and emerging on Sturdies Bay Road at the head of Whaler Bay just a little north of Burrill Road. From this point the ferry is only a short distance along the road to the right.

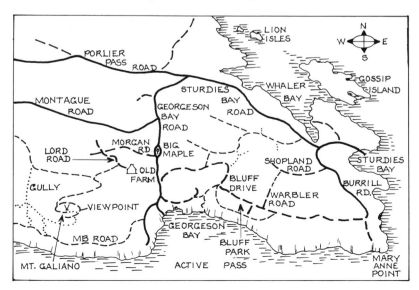

SQUAMISH-CHEAKAMUS

28 ELFIN LAKES

Round trip 23 km (14 mi)
Allow 8 hours
High point 1650 m (5400 ft)
Elevation gain 730 m (2400 ft)
Best July to mid October
Maps Squamish 92G/11,
Cheakamus River 92G/14

Although the Diamond Head Lodge is gone, you may still stay overnight in the shelter hut erected by Provincial Parks if you wish to spend more than one day in this scenic area. You have to carry in food and sleeping bag, of course, and a tent too if you prefer to camp.

To reach the start of this trail, bypass Squamish on Highway 99, cross Mamquam River, and some 500 metres beyond the bridge turn sharp right on Mamquam Road. The road first parallels the river, rising steadily, then climbs by way of a fairly sharp left fork (signposted). From here, the going is rough in spots but is generally quite passable if you take your time and exercise caution. Ample parking is available at the gate with its visitor register some 16 km (10 mi) from the highway.

From here, a rough road first heads north, then switchbacks high on the south side of Mashiter Creek, first through open forest, then over the semi-alpine Red Heather Meadows, rising steadily to just below the high point of Paul Ridge. It is possible, however, to cut off some of the lower bends by using a foot-trail, the original route: go right and uphill, following markers

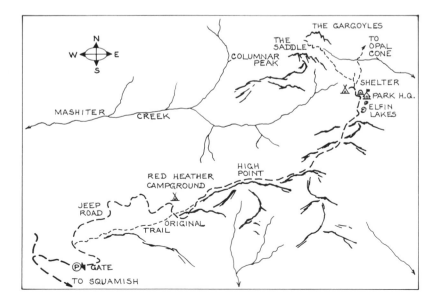

Diamond Head area and Elfin Lakes

and tapes after about 20 minutes from the gate. By so doing, you reduce your distance by some 3 km (2 mi).

The high point makes a good resting place with breathtaking views: Mount Garibaldi towers on the north, Mamquam's sprawling bulk dominates the east, away to the south are the pointed summits of Habrich and Sky Pilot, and the Squamish valley has a spectacular backdrop in the summits of the Tantalus Range.

From the ridge, a gentle descent of 150 m (500 ft) leads to the shelter, set beside the little lakes, with the campground in the meadow below. For many, this is enough; for those who wish to explore farther, there are the Gargoyles, Little Diamond Head, for properly equipped groups the Garibaldi glacier, and for climbers, Garibaldi itself. A trail also goes east towards Opal Cone and Mamquam Lake.

In winter the area is beautiful but somewhat difficult of access because of the steep approach road. The very best time for a visit is probably late July through August when the snow has receded and the meadows are at their most brilliant, for the cold relaxes its grip slowly in the area, and patches of white greet the hiker from the sweltering city till quite late in the summer months. A park ranger is now stationed here in summer, headquartered in the one-time lodge—many older Vancouverites will have fond memories of it and of its owners, the Brandvolds.

SQUAMISH-CHEAKAMUS

29 MAMQUAM LAKE

Round trip 24 km (15 mi)
Allow 9 hours
High point 1525 m (5000 ft)
Elevation change 610 m (2000 ft)
Best late July to September
Map Western Mamquam Mountain
92G/15

One of the most rewarding hiking trips from Elfin Lakes takes you across Ring Creek and past Opal Cone (1710 m or 5600 ft) to this lake, beautifully situated at the foot of Pyramid Mountain. Check with the ranger, however, before you set out on the improved trail to find out whether Skookum Creek is passable; in hot weather it may run high with glacial meltwater.

A short distance beyond the Elfin Lakes shelter, a sign points right for Mamquam Lake (going left takes you to the Saddle and an unmarked route to Little Diamond Head), and at first you descend on an easy grade into the valley of Ring Creek with its steep lateral moraine sides. Cross the creek, and once on the east bank continue north for a short distance before your route swings back and ascends the valley sidewall, bringing you to Opal Cone meadows. To climb to the crater rim of this extinct volcano, you may go left here and follow the steep grassy slope upward; alternatively, you may continue on the main trail to the next lateral moraine, then swing left and follow it to the point where you can ascend to the ridge north and east of the peak, for a round trip of about 13 km (8 mi).

The main trail continues eastward, crossing the kind of lunar landscape associated with areas recently glaciated. Then it descends to the valley of the west branch of Skookum Creek before rising again on the other side to

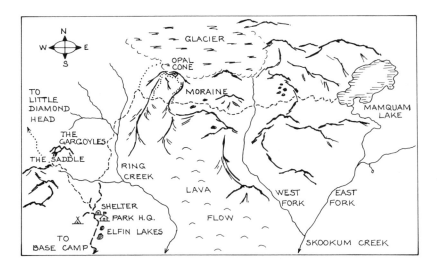

Across the barrens to Pyramid Mountain

the small glacial lakes called Rampart Ponds. Finally you reach the view of Mamquam Lake, 250 m (820 ft) below you, with the trail switchbacking down to it. You can, of course, if you are making this a backpacking trip, camp at the ponds and go down unladen to sample the fishing, with rainbow trout a feature.

Although this is a longish one-day trip, the Provincial Parks personnel are improving the trail, and you do have the alternative of Opal Cone for a shorter hike that gives fine views of Bishop Glacier and the mountains north and west of Mount Garibaldi, as well as of the Big One itself.

SQUAMISH-CHEAKAMUS

30 HIGH FALLS CREEK

Round trip 12 km (7.5 mi)
Allow 5 hours
High point 715 m (2350 ft)
Elevation gain 640 m (2100 ft)
Best May to November
Map Cheakamus River 92G/14

Do not be misled by the moderate-looking statistics associated with this outing. The trail ascends steeply on bluffs above the falls in its early stages, though a fixed plastic cable is now in place to help you. Another point: if you feel sufficiently interested to try this hike, choose a clear, sunny day, for its views are superb: of the falls themselves, of the Tantalus Range to the southwest, and on the return trip, of the upper Squamish and the peaks between the river and Ashlu Creek.

To reach the beginning, drive on Highway 99 to the Alice Lake Park sign and go left opposite it on the road for Cheekye. There pass Fergie's Fishing Lodge, cross the Cheakamus River and continue straight ahead for 18.7 km (11.7 mi) up the wide valley of the Squamish River to the Weldwood Company's gate, where you may have to check in. Proceed another 4.4 km (2.7 mi) and park just beyond the High Falls Creek crossing, where an old logging road goes off right.

Walk along this for a short distance, then swing right towards the bluffs that the trail ascends, keeping the creek on your right and below you. After about an hour of steady climbing comes your first viewpoint of the falls, particularly spectacular in the late spring runoff when a rainbow gives a halo effect to the great downpouring of water. From here, more steady climbing brings you to a bluff with a variety of views of surrounding peaks as well as of the braided main river in its U-shaped valley.

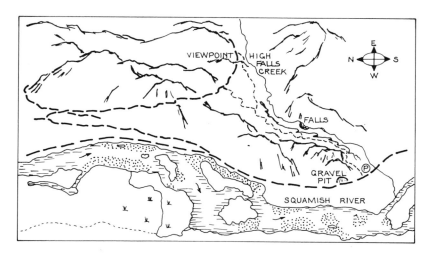

View up the Squamish River from the logging road

The original taped route bore left through mature forest away from the creek; a new one, however, remains closer to the stream finally crossing a recent cutover before emerging on a logging road a little beyond its high point. Turn back left here to make the road your return route as an alternative to scrambling down the bluffs.

The superb views up the Squamish are provided on your return via the logging road as it heads down a clear sidehill on its descent to the main valley floor. From the junction with the main logging access road, a walk of some 1.4 km (0.9 mi) brings you back to your transportation and the end of your hike.

SQUAMISH-CHEAKAMUS

31 ALICE RIDGE

Round trip (ridge only) 8 km (5 mi)
Allow 5 hours
High point 2075 m (6800 ft)
Elevation gain 700 m (2300 ft)
Best July to October

Round trip (including road) up to
    26 km (16 mi)
Allow up to 10 hours
Elevation gain up to 1405 m (4600 ft)
Best June to October
Map Cheakamus River 92G/14

The greatest deterrent to this trip is not natural but results from the deterioration of the vehicle approach, involving you in a longer or shorter walk on a logging road depending on the state of your car and your own determination. Still, if you can reach the fork 7.7 km (4.8 mi) beyond the Alice Lake Park Headquarters, you will soon find yourself above the forest, with striking views from the road across the Squamish valley to the Tantalus Range and south to the Habrich—Sky Pilot group.

Follow Highway 99 north for 6.8 km (4.3 mi) from the traffic light at Squamish and go right at the sign for Alice Lake Provincial Park. At its entrance, stay left but take the right fork where the road splits at Park Headquarters and continue on this gravel road past its intersection with Four Lakes Trail between Fawn and Edith lakes. Next you cross a powerline right-of-way, and thereafter your road starts to climb, becoming bumpy in the process. Your rule now, with one exception, is left forks all the way.

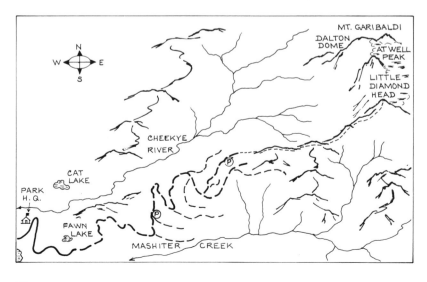

Dalton Dome and Atwell Peak

After several long switchbacks, you finally crest at 1220 m (4000 ft) and now comes the exception to the stay-left rule; a pole sign directs you to the right. At the next fork, however, it is left again, and if you have come a fair part of the way to this point on foot, a satisfying destination may be an outlying spur a little to the right of the road with a rough track leading up to it. If, however, you are pressing on for the ridge, you stay with the road, which first rises then descends a little around the north end of the outlier, finally culminating in the trail proper.

This continues steadily upward, at first among trees, later in the open where tapes cease, but the ridge is by this time sufficiently narrow to make route-finding simple as it rises to Little Diamond Head. This point makes a fine climax for a day hike; to the north looms the mass of Mount Garibaldi, and elsewhere the land falls away to reveal more mountains and valleys, with the town of Squamish lying in the midst of them.

Those wishing a longer trip or considering a backpacking expedition may head for the open country around Elfin Lakes Campground by dropping almost due south past the Gargoyles to the Saddle and thus to the shelter, a distance of some 5 km (3 mi). Obviously this more than doubles the length of the round trip, and logistic experts may be tempted to work out a cross-country route to Base Camp at the end of the Elfin Lakes Trail (Hike 28). They should keep in mind, however, that their vehicle is now at the end of a logging road some 32 km (20 mi) off, a thought that may suggest return by the original route.

Garibaldi Lake and Battleship Islands – *D. Ellis*

SQUAMISH-CHEAKAMUS

32 GARIBALDI LAKE

Round trip 17.5 km (11 mi)
Allow 6 hours
High point 1555 m (5100 ft)
Elevation gain 885 m (2900 ft)
Best July to mid October
Map Cheakamus River 92G/14

Although many visitors will want to spend a few days exploring the numerous features of Garibaldi Provincial Park's western section, the lake itself may be the destination for a one-day hiking trip into this country of alpine meadows with their profusion of wild flowers, evidence of past volcanic activity, mountain lakes, peaks and glaciers. In any case, the trail passes the Taylor Campground, which may well be the starting point for other trips.

To reach the start of the trail, drive north from Squamish on Highway 99 for nearly 37 km (23 mi) to the settlement of Garibaldi. Just under 2 km (1.2 mi) after the Garibaldi Station turnoff on the left, a sign indicating the Black Tusk Recreation Area points off to the right; from here a short paved road leads to Rubble Creek parking lot and the start of hiking. The well-graded trail zigzags upward parallel to the creek, and to the left of the great natural lava wall, the Barrier. The viewpoint across from this feature makes an appropriate destination in itself for a short day trip. Before that, however, is a fork, left to Taylor Campground—the suggested route—and right to Barrier Lake.

After a hike of nearly 3 hours comes the campground, where signs point out routes to various destinations; obviously, you will take the one to the main lake, which is also the site of the Park Headquarters. There you may contemplate the vivid colouring of the glacial water and the surrounding mountains before returning, this time staying left to Lesser Garibaldi Lake and Barrier Lake (Barrier drains underground into what eventually makes its reappearance as Rubble Creek). Next, turn off left for the viewpoint overlooking the Barrier before returning to the fork and the trail down to your car.

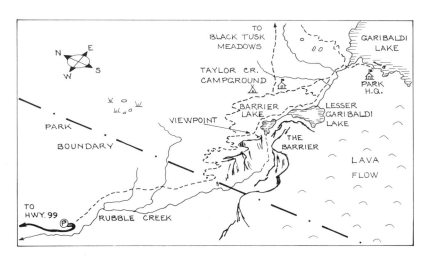

SQUAMISH-CHEAKAMUS

33 PANORAMA RIDGE

Round trip (from the campground 10 km (6.2 mi)
Allow 4 hours
High point 2250 m (7400 ft)
Elevation gain 700 m (2300 ft)
Best late July to early October
Map Cheakamus River 92G/14

The trip to the prominent alpine feature of Garibaldi Park's Black Tusk area takes you northeast from the Taylor Campground. You follow Mimulus Lake Trail for a start, then stay right at the first fork, which has a directional sign, and cross Mimulus Creek. Fork right again and head upward and eastward, travelling north of and more or less parallel to Garibaldi Lake as you ascend—note the naval force on its waters, the Battleship Islands. The ridge itself has a number of false summits, each with its distinctive view, but the highest point is easily identified by the presence of a large rock cairn.

From here, your views are superb: the intense blue-green water of the main lake at your feet contrasts with the gleaming white of Mount Garibaldi's glaciers and snowfields. You also have the whole variety of volcanic features as outlined in W. H. Mathews's short study, **Garibaldi Geology:** Table Mountain and the quaintly named Phyllis's Engine, for instance, with Mount Price and Clinker Peak almost directly opposite you across the lake. All are mute reminders of a period of intense igneous activity, quite recent on the geological time scale. Northward, you look across towards Whistler Mountain and, of course, Black Tusk stands up proudly in the northwest.

This hike can be accomplished as a strenuous day trip from the parking lot; it is much pleasanter, though, to do it from Taylor or from Lake campground. From one of these places, you may enjoy it as a gentle hike, giving

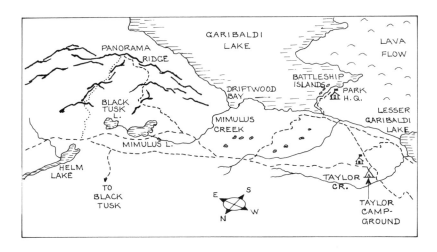

Garibaldi Lake from the summit – *D. Ellis*

yourself time to take in the magnificent scenery and savour the silence of the mountains from your lofty perch. Note that, if you have a fair sense of direction and the weather is clear, you may vary your return route by working from the summit in a generally northerly direction along a ridge that brings you down to the east of Black Tusk Lake.

Here you meet the main trail, on which you turn left and pass to the west of Mimulus Lake as you head back to camp. Do heed the signs that ask you to remain on the trail so that others may enjoy the flowers of the alpine meadows in the short summer season.

Note: BC Parks has decided to close the route described and has developed a trail east of Mimulus Lake approximately following the return route suggested above. Please watch for signs directing you to this new trail.

Black Tusk from the meadows
– D. Ellis

34 BLACK TUSK

Round trip 12 km (7.5 mi)
Allow 5 hours
High point 2315 m (7600 ft)
Elevation gain 790 m (2580 ft)
Best late July to early October
Map Cheakamus River 92G/14

This is another trip that you will want to devote a good part of your day to, so much is there to see and enjoy, both along the trail and on the peak itself. The one drawback to the outing is the fact that the only way up the last stretch to the crown of the Tusk is by a narrow chimney involving a climb of about 100 m (330 ft). For this reason, you should go with a properly organized party, and a rope might not come amiss. One other warning: watch for falling rock if other climbers are ahead of you.

The route starts on the Upper Lakes Trail, going left at a major intersection just beyond the crossing of Parnassus Creek. You thus bypass Mimulus Lake and the smaller Black Tusk Lake before bearing left again towards

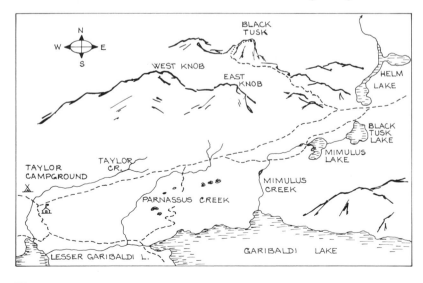

Black Tusk from Panorama Ridge— *D. Ellis*

the objective—first over alpine meadows, later across the talus that so plentifully surrounds the great pillar towering above. Just east of the Tusk proper is a saddle that may serve as a destination for the inexperienced or the ill-equipped; if you are going all the way, however, continue westward under the almost vertical south wall, passing several chimneys as you go. The last of these provides the only ascent that is relatively safe, and it is here that the trail ends.

Handholds in the chimney are numerous and safe; the rock formation, too, gives some protection from exposure. Be careful to note the route once you reach the top to ensure that you return by the same one after you have enjoyed the sublime view from the high point: the park itself laid out before you with Helm Lake and its forbidding Cinder Flats almost at your feet and, farther off, the upper part of the valley of the Cheakamus River dominated by the great bulk of the mountain chain running east from Whistler. Then, as you turn westward, you look across a lower stretch of the same water after it has made its big bend to the south and before it suffers the indignity of a B.C. Hydro dam at its outlet from Daisy Lake.

SQUAMISH-CHEAKAMUS

35 EMPETRUM PEAK

Round trip 14 km (9 mi)
Allow 6 hours
High point 1990 m (6530 ft)
Elevation gain 425 m (1400 ft)
Best late July to early October
Map Cheakamus River 92G/14

This hike takes you north of Black Tusk, and the round trip is a full day's outing, even starting from the campground. Upper Lakes Trail provides the route for the first part of your journey. Go north along it, taking the left fork and passing to the west of Mimulus Lake and its smaller neighbour, Black Tusk Lake, as you rise to the main north-south divide. From here your view to the north is of Helm Lake and its outlet creek, a tributary of the Cheakamus River. A trail follows the creek's course on the east side, providing access to the high country from the north and allowing for a possible crossover—one-day or backpack—if you are with a two-car party (see Hike 38).

Before you reach the lake, leave the main Helm Creek Trail and keep to the left side of this narrow body of water until you round the end of the ridge, while looking across to Cinder Cone and its flats on the opposite side. From the lake, strike off northwest; soon the country begins to open out and you see the ridge ahead. Its west side is very steep, but the ascent from the southeast—your approach—is relatively simple by an ascending traverse. Follow the ridge to its high point with its striking view of Black Tusk, then look to the west for the summits and icefields of the great mountain chain that separates the Cheakamus (after it has turned south) from the valley of the Squamish River.

Below you on the east is the valley of Helm Creek, though its other title

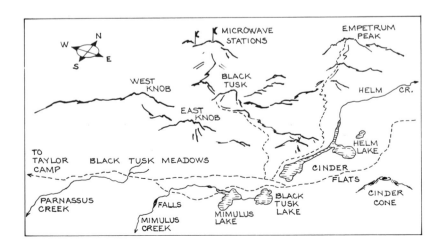

Dramatic view of Black Tusk from Empetrum Ridge—*D. Ellis*

—Desolation Valley—seems more appropriate, as it is strewn with volcanic debris that makes it a barren foreground to the icefields of Helm Glacier. North of the tributary valley is the Cheakamus River, flowing from the lake of the same name, and Whistler Mountain once more supplies the background.

There is an austerity about this scene, perhaps because its main outlook is to the north, that may send you back to camp in a somewhat chastened mood. On the other hand, here is a suitably strenuous adventure trip to wind up your stay in this picturesque section of Garibaldi Park.

Phlox and lichens

36 BREW LAKE

Round trip 13 km (8 mi)
Allow 7 hours
High point 1420 m (4650 ft)
Elevation gain 1020 m (3350 ft)
Best July to October
Map Brandywine 92J/3

Your approach to this trail differs from the usual: it lies along the B.C. Railway track, heading south from the point where Highway 99, en route to Whistler, crosses it from east to west just south of Brandywine Falls Provincial Park, a suitable parking spot. From here (the right-of-way is wide, but watch for trains, especially silent Dayliners) walk back along the line for approximately 25 minutes to where it makes a right-angled bend to the west, goes under the Hydro powerline, then turns back sharp south. A short distance beyond this last direction change, on the south side of a small creek,

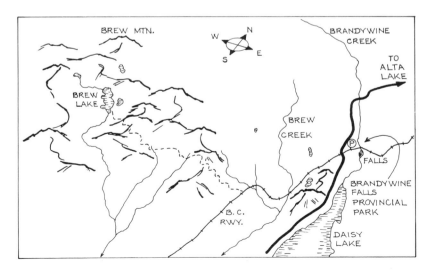

Tricouni Mountain from the ridge above Brew Lake – *R. Edgell*

the trail heads off to the west, marked with aluminum squares and orange markers.

At first you rise through open forest, but later come rocky slopes and talus slides. As you climb, you find the route crossing various ridges or working around them. The footing, too, changes, becoming rocky in the higher reaches; still, the route is well defined now that UBC's Varsity Outdoor Club has taken responsibility for its maintenance, and some of the steeper ridge crossings have been modified by trail building.

On gentler stretches, there are blueberries; the upper part of the trail, in fact, tends to be bushy in spring, but annual clearing has helped. The lake, in a rock basin, is reputed to contain fish; you may use its shore for an overnight camp if you want to tackle Brew Mountain (1740 m/5700 ft) or follow one of the ridges between the valleys of the Cheakamus and the Squamish.

SQUAMISH-CHEAKAMUS

37 BRANDYWINE MEADOWS

Round trip 10 km (6.2 mi)
Allow 4 hours
High point 1420 m (4650 ft)
Elevation gain 670 m (2200 ft)
Best July to October
Map Brandywine 92J/3

Cessation of major mining and logging activity in the lower valley has reopened the approach road to public use and now permits much easier access than before, albeit at the expense of the lower part of the trail. For experienced groups, Brandywine Mountain or Metaldome are possible in a day, but for less ambitious mortals the subalpine and alpine meadows provide sufficient reward.

Taking Brandywine Falls Provincial Park as a reference point if you are travelling north on Highway 99, you turn off left on a logging road just 2.7 km (1.7 mi) beyond the park at B.C. Hydro Tower 64.2. Follow this road for 4.5 km (2.8 mi) to where a gate bars your onward progress, Mount Fee providing an eye-filling spectacle ahead. At the gate, you take the middle road, BR 10, and proceed along it for about 30 minutes, gradually ascending and passing through the first band of trees that breaks the monotony of logged-off areas. In the second band, a substantial tributary stream lies just beyond the well-marked trail that comes uphill from the left, a relic of earlier days when the hiking trail started much lower down on Brandywine Creek itself.

You turn right, however, and immediately you start rising steeply along the east side of the creek with some windfalls to negotiate en route. Next you approach a logged-over patch with its debris; however, you remain

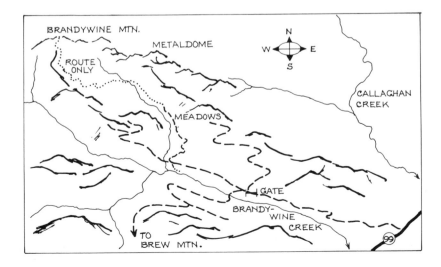

Looking from the meadows towards Brandywine Mountain

within the margin of trees as the grade eases, and you negotiate a few damp spots before you start rising again towards the meadows lying at and above the treeline.

Here, though snow lies late, from the end of July through September the meadows bloom, but, as in every Eden, there are drawbacks—damp spots early in the season and insects to contend with. If, of course, your eyes are set on higher things, an intermittent trail continues towards Brandywine Mountain, the approach to which is relatively clear. Remember, though, that you are letting yourself in for another 690 m (2260 ft) of climbing, with an extra 3 hours or so on the trail.

SQUAMISH-CHEAKAMUS

38 HELM CREEK TRAIL

Round trip 24 km (15 mi)
Allow 8 hours
High point 1740 m (5700 ft)
Elevation gain 915 m (3000 ft)
Best July to October
Maps Brandywine 92J/3,
Alta Lake 92J/2

B.C. Provincial Parks is responsible for this interesting alternative approach to the high country around Helm Lake and the Black Tusk, via a most attractive and well-graded trail. One warning, though. At least two people, perhaps three, are necessary to operate the cable-car crossing of the swift-flowing Cheakamus River about 1.5 km (1 mi) from the starting point.

The hike begins at the Cheakamus Lake parking lot, about 7 km (4.5 mi) from Highway 99. This point is reached by turning east off the highway at the Cheakamus Lake marker a short distance after the road has crossed to the right of the B.C. Railway track and turned north towards Whistler. After a little over 400 metres, stay left at a fork, then remain with the travelled road which, though rather rough, is quite drivable. Soon after you have started walking comes the Garibaldi Park entrance with its hiker registration sheet; then you travel through a fine forest for about 30 minutes.

Now comes a sign announcing the trail, pointing right towards the river. Drop down to the bank and face the cable-car crossing. Once across, the route zigzags steadily uphill, working back towards the creek, the sound of

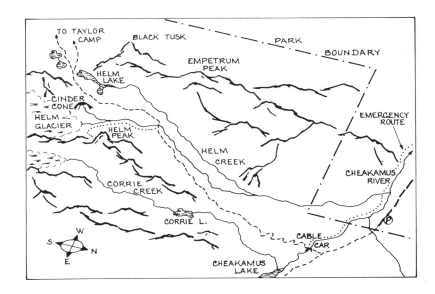

Cable car across Cheakamus River

which becomes audible as you approach. At last the grade eases off as the trail enters the open forest of the wide upper valley. In this you remain, the main creek on your right, and as the trees thin out, you have a fine series of views: Helm Peak to the left, Cinder Cone front left, Black Tusk front right and Empetrum Ridge right.

As you ascend, the country opens up, and finally, as you breast the final rise, the lake lies spread out before you. Here is a destination for most hikers, though some will undoubtedly wish to try one of the surrounding heights. There is also the chance of a crossover, but that is for experienced walkers travelling as a group and with transport arranged at the Black Tusk approach (Hike 32).

Rainbow Lake from the west— *D. Ellis*

WHISTLER

39 RAINBOW LAKE

Round trip 18 km (11 mi)
Allow 6.5 hours
High point 1465 m (4800 ft)
Elevation gain 825 m (2700 ft)
Best July to October
Maps Alta Lake 92J/2,
    Brandywine 92J/3

With the development of Whistler into a year-round recreation resort, it is fitting that summer visitors to the area should have a good choice of outings into the high country on either side of the valley. Two or three of these can be reached from Twenty-one Mile Creek, which stretches off to the northwest and gives the choice of an easy day at Rainbow Lake, a sidetrip to other lakes in a tributary valley, or for the energetic, an ascent of Rainbow Mountain.

About 2.5 km (1.5 mi) beyond the B.C. Railway crossing as you approach Whistler from the south, you turn left off Highway 99 onto Alta Lake Road.

Having recrossed the railway track, you travel along the west side of the valley for 7 km (4.3 mi) to where the road crosses Twenty-one Mile Creek for the start of the trail. On the way, notice the one-time approach to this hike, an old road diverging gradually from yours to the left close to a B.C. Hydro tower. Nowadays, you start on the south bank of the creek itself, your trail the product of a public-spirited effort by the Whistler Rotary Club.

At first you ascend quite steeply, accompanied by the sound of rushing water on your right, and soon you are treated to views of two sets of falls, the lower visible from the trail, the upper a little beyond the point where you start climbing up to the benchland on which you now go forward, the old road from the left linking up with your route. From now on you continue upstream, your way indicated by orange markers through first a logged-off area, now regenerating, then fine old forest. Finally you reach a swampy area and, though some improvements have been made, you may still find wet spots here in the early summer. The crossing of Twenty-one Mile Creek, just before you reach the alpine basin that contains your objective, may also be awkward if the bridge has had one of its misadventures.

These drawbacks aside, it is a fine trail leading to an area from which a number of other excursions are quite feasible. Rainbow Mountain itself is an easy ascent; continue west along the length of the lake before striking upward to the ridge west of the peak. Another possibility is the short sidetrip to Gin and Tonic lakes, reached by turning left off the main trail before it crosses Twenty-one Mile Creek and heading up the valley to the west. From Tonic Lake, if you are really enthusiastic, you may make for Sproatt Ridge with its panoramic views.

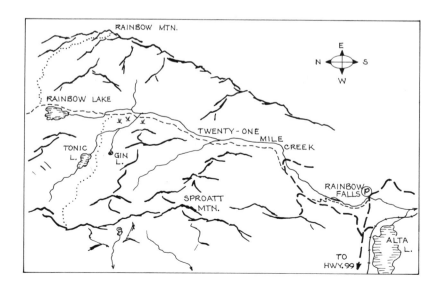

40 ALPINE WHISTLER

Round trip (to Oboe) 12 km (7.5 mi)
Allow 7 hours
High point 2130 m (6990 ft)
Elevation gain 505 m (1660 ft)

Round trip (crossover) 15 km (9 mi)
Allow 7 hours
High point 2130 m (6990 ft)
Elevation gain 300 m (980 ft)
Best late July to October
Map Alta Lake 92J/2

For this hike it is necessary that the Whistler lifts be operating, so you should first check with the Whistler Information Centre (tel. 932-5528). The great advantage of starting close to your high point is that you leave yourself a number of options: along the "Musical Bumps" and return, a shorter hike up Whistler Mountain itself and return, or either of these combined with a hike down the ski trails leading back to Gondola Base.

From the valley floor you enjoy a ride up the mountain, first by gondola, then on the Red Chair. The latter decants you close to the Roundhouse on the mountain's north shoulder, with the peak of Whistler Mountain across the great bowl to your right. You start uphill half right on an improved track then, after some 15 minutes, you work left to the top of the T-bar on a steepish sidehill. Next you pass along at the foot of two talus slopes, then ease up towards the main ridge, avoiding as much as possible the icy patches below the minor summit (unofficially called Little Whistler) southeast of the main peak. On Whistler itself the world opens out, and you may enjoy views of mountains stretching in all directions—and all this for a hike of only 6.5 km (4 mi).

Closer to hand, however, pointing southeast towards Overlord Mountain and its glacier, runs a ridge which makes an enjoyable hike on its own or in combination with the one to Whistler. For this, you begin by following the Whistler Mountain route from the Roundhouse, but after passing Little Whistler bear left and head in a southeasterly direction along the ridge. Now you enjoy glorious open hiking as you go over the "Musical Bumps," Piccolo, Flute and Oboe descending in succession from one to the other so that by the time you reach the last you are 220 m (720 ft) lower than when you started. Here you are above the meadows at Singing Pass, 190 m (625 ft) below you.

Now is a good time to turn if you wish to go back by the high route, but yet another option is possible. With a previously organized car, you may opt to descend the long flower slope to Singing Pass and join the Fitzsimmons Creek Trail for your return (Hike 41).

Cheakamus Lake from Whistler Mountain – *D. Ellis*

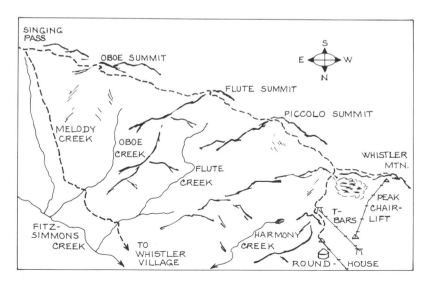

93

WHISTLER

41 RUSSET LAKE

Round trip 18 km (11 mi)
Allow 8 hours
High point 1950 m (6400 ft)
Elevation gain 850 m (2800 ft)
Best late July to October
Map Alta Lake 92J/2

"Oh ye'll tak' the high road, and I'll tak' the low road" seems an appropriate sentiment for the two approaches to this scenic alpine area. The high road is, of course, the route over the "Musical Bumps" to Singing Pass (Hike 40), where we join it for the last stretch to Russet Lake, a fine centre for wilderness hiking and climbing. The low road is by Fitzsimmons Creek, which has had an interesting history as your approach road testifies, its having served a logging operation as well as a gold mine in the days before its upper stretches were incorporated in Garibaldi Park and an improved trail built along the south side of the valley.

To reach your start point, you travel about 2.5 km (1.5 mi) north on Highway 99 from the Gondola Base to the new Whistler village, going off right on Village Gate Way and right again on Blackcomb Way. As you travel along this thoroughfare, keep an eye out for the rough-looking Singing Pass approach road also going off to the right (if you cross Fitzsimmons Creek, you have missed your turnoff). On this dirt road you start to rise, doubling back left past a water tower where the Whistler Control Road bears right, then heading up into the valley of the creek for nearly 5 km (3 mi) to the parking space at the trailhead. Here you are requested to

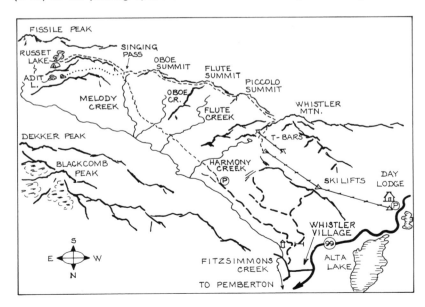

In the meadows at Singing Pass— *D. Ellis*

register because you are going into rugged alpine country, with no services available.

On the trail itself, you very soon come on the tailings that have toppled down the slope from the mine, then you continue eastward in forest high above Fitzsimmons Creek, crossing Harmony, Flute and Oboe creeks until you reach treeline, and then you swing south into the valley of Melody Creek. Now the meadows begin, a mass of colour in season—but these fragile meadows must be protected, so stay on the trail as you cross the wet spots on your way to Singing Pass at the head of the valley. Here you are greeted by the unforgettable sight of Cheakamus Lake, seemingly at your feet so steep is the drop-off; and there opposite is the Black Tusk, with Mount Garibaldi farther away and to its left.

But you have to reach your destination so, shouldering your pack, you make for Russet Lake and the B.C. Mountaineering Club cabin, traversing up around the east side of a knoll before dropping again to the lake, which lies about 2.5 km (1.5 mi) from the pass. At your destination you are in the sublimity of the alpine, with Fissile Peak frowning above you and the glaciers of the Spearhead Range across the valley to the northeast.

Nor are you denied views on the return trip. Once you are back above Fitzsimmons Creek, you are looking across the main valley to Rainbow and the peaks on its western side. Who is to blame you if you become a little blasé about mountain views?

WHISTLER

42 WEDGEMOUNT LAKE

Round trip 14 km (8.7 mi)
Allow 8 hours
High point 1920 m (6300 ft)
Elevation gain 1220 m (4000 ft)
Best July to September
Map Alta Lake 92J/2

A spectacular glacial lake lying in the shadow of Weart Mountain serves as the destination of this hike. The approach is via Highway 99, with a right turnoff across the B.C. Railway tracks to a parking and trip registration area just by the Green River, 11.5 km (7 mi) north of the Whistler village traffic light as you travel towards Pemberton. At first you are on a broad gravel road that goes left just across the river then passes to the right of a large sand pit. At the first fork, go right on a logging road, and shortly thereafter left on an old road that has deteriorated almost to trail status. Here you have a rich ground cover of moss on your right before you emerge from the forest onto a logged-over area with bluffs on your right, a mantling of shattered rock at their foot.

Your next fork is to the left as well, your route this time marked by a cairn. The road here is somewhat overgrown at present, as is the case at the next point of decision, where you go right, following a stone arrow and a post with tapes, the same being true when your trail just before Wedgemount Creek is marked by small cairns and more tape. Next, 3.2 km (2 mi) from your start, comes the creek crossing, in two parts on two log bridges (don't forget to release your backpack straps). Now you ascend a small spire on

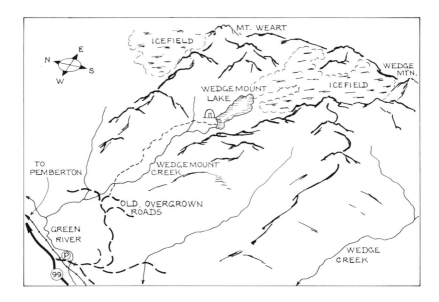

Wedgemount shelter and campsite— *S. Werner*

the north bank, heading into the forest; from here continue eastward, remaining parallel to but well above the channel as you rise.

This trail is steep—very steep—and you climb 1200 m (3940 ft) in less than 6 km (3.7 mi). Fortunately there are a few easier stretches, though the first is a good way along, probably beyond the point at which the average frail human will want to draw breath. This spot is also the first with a reliable water supply.

The forest is thick on the lower reaches of the trail; later, however, trees thin out and you are delighted by spectacular views of Wedgemount Creek dropping some 300 m (980 ft) in a cloud of white spray. For the final third of the hike, you are on heathery alpine meadows, but remember that snow stays late, often lingering into July, so you should probably save this trip until late summer.

The beautifully sited lake has the foot of a glacier at its upper end and great snowfields standing above it to the east. At the lake is a B.C. Mountaineering Club cabin, open to climbers, and there is also a small wilderness campsite. Mountain goats may be seen on the high ridges, as may alpinists making for the snowclad peaks.

PEMBERTON

43 TENQUILLE LAKE

Round trip (long) 19 km (12 mi)
Allow 8 hours
High point 1710 m (5600 ft)
Elevation gain 1460 m (4800 ft)

Round trip (short) 12 km (7.5 mi)
Allow 5 hours
Elevation gain 458 m (1500 ft)
Best July to October
Map Birkenhead Lake 92J/10

This scenic trip, culminating in splendid alpine meadows around the lake, takes you northwest from Pemberton following the Lillooet River upstream in its wide fertile valley dotted with farms. To reach the trailhead, follow the Pemberton Meadows road for 23.5 km (14.6 mi) from the village, then turn right at the Tenquille Lake sign and cross to the river's north bank. Here you must choose whether to hike the whole way from a trail beginning just to the right of the bridge, or have a vehicle do some of the work for you by driving up the once infamous Hurley Road towards Bralorne.

For the purist hiker, parking is just off the road to the right of the bridge beyond a Forest Service trail sign. At first your marked route zigzags uphill to the east, merges with the original trail coming up from the right, then turns back north. Your way lies through open forest, giving you tantalizing glimpses of the rich valley below and the peaks opposite. En route you cross several small streams (possibly dry in late summer), then work into the valley of the Wolverine, finally crossing the creek at about 1500 m (5000 ft), at which height the trees have become sparser and you have al-

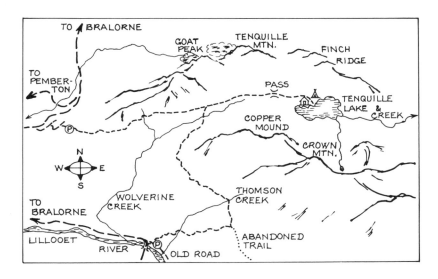

Sun God from Tenquille Lake

ready traversed some small meadows. Shortly thereafter, the alternative trail joins from the left for the last few hundred feet of climbing to the meadows above the lake.

To reach the latter approach, go left after crossing the Lillooet River, drive upstream for 7.4 km (4.6 mi) then turn right on the new Hurley Road, noting at the 6.2 km (3.9 mi) mark the original road, now passable only by 4WD vehicles. Stay with the new road for 10.9 km (6.8 mi) to where the original Hurley joins from the right. Here turn sharp right back along the old road for 2.2 km (1.4 mi) then go left up a steep hill. On this now very eroded road, fork right after 2 km (1.3 mi) and right again shortly thereafter to reach the parking place at the end of the road, nearly 24 km (15 mi) in all from the Lillooet River bridge.

Here the trail begins, heading through logging slash to the edge of the forest, in which the grade eases and there is only one creek crossing on two springy logs to provide excitement until you reach the junction with the old trail. Beyond this point you pass through rich meadows, lush with flowers of many kinds and colours, which give way to smaller, more modest plants and heather as you approach the high point before the trail drops down again to the lake. Here a small cabin and a number of campsites testify to the popularity of the lake with backpackers. There is alleged to be fishing, or you may inspect old mining claims, and various hikes are possible: Copper Mound to the south, its ridge leading to Sun God in the southeast, with Goat Peak and Tenquille Mountain to west and north.

44 TENQUILLE CREEK

Round trip (to lakes) 11 km (7 mi)
Allow 5 hours
High point 1675 m (5500 ft)
Elevation gain 427 m (1400 ft)
Best late July to October
Map Birkenhead 92J/10

Here's an outing for the venturesome driver/hiker on an old mining pack trail, recently cleared of most of its windfalls and, as a result, providing a well-marked route. The one drawback, if it is one, is that nearly all the reward comes at the end with a pair of delightful little lakes, a decaying cabin by the lower one recalling B.C.'s mining past, when the mineral deposits of this area were worked in the 1920s. Getting there, however, involves some effort, with a longish walk in forest to start with and most of your height gain reserved for late in the trip when you ascend a scree slope reached by a taped route between an old rock slide and a fresh avalanche path.

Before this, however, you drive up the Birkenhead River from the point where you depart left from the road to D'Arcy, 16.5 km (10.3 mi) north of the Mount Currie T-junction, a notice at the beginning announcing that this road does not give access to Birkenhead Lake Provincial Park, perhaps because of the logging traffic on it. In any event, you cross the railway, swing right, then left as you start your climb out of the main valley, eventually emerging with the river far below on your left, and to your front some stark mountain

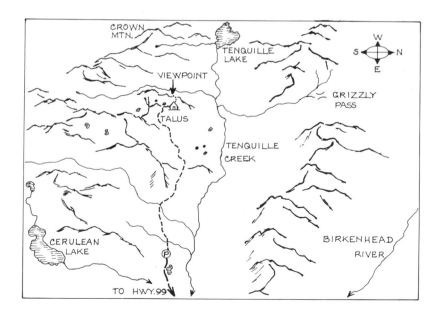

Tenquille Lake and Mountain from the ridge

peaks, their red and orange flanks denoting mineralization.

After 10.8 km (6.7 mi) you go left, cross the main river on a smart Bailey bridge and begin your climb into the valley of Tenquille Creek, with an interesting canyon for a passenger to stare down into, if he is not sitting with his eyes shut. Although the road deteriorates somewhat, it poses no real problems, and one reward for being on it is the sight of a lovely little lake, its waters opalescent and reflective, situated about 1.4 km (0.9 mi) before the present road ends, 7 km (4.5 mi) from the bridge.

To start the walking part of your trip, you cross a creek, then follow a cat road for 10 minutes, from which point you are on the old pack trail, its age testified to by two moss-covered bridges. To be fair, you do suffer a little of the soul-purging of Mountain Misery (white rhododendron) here and there, so don't wear shorts, but that unpleasantness is left behind when you emerge from forest at the foot of the rock slide, with the sheared-off trees of the recent avalanche ahead. There is, however, a perfectly negotiable stretch between the two just after you have crossed a little creek.

Follow the tapes uphill from here until you come on the old pack trail again, now switchbacking across a scree slope and heading for a prominent shoulder a little to the right. Breast the final slope and you are at the lower of the two lakes, the old cabin by its shore. To enlarge your field of view, head up the ridge behind the cabin for some 95 m (300 ft), from which point you look across the upper valley, with Tenquille Lake itself somewhat to the right and lower than your vantage point.

On this trip, the imagination may play with the thought of the pack animals making for the Li-Li-Kel Company's operation, and if you are returning near sunset, give the driver a chance to share the sight of exotically coloured ridges instead of his having to listen with envy to the exclamations of his passengers.

First view of the waterfall

PEMBERTON

45 PLACE GLACIER TRAIL

Round trip 21 km (13 mi)
Allow 9 hours
High point 1830 m (6000 ft)
Elevation gain 1373 m (4500 ft)
Best July to October
Map Pemberton 92J/7

The Scots admonition to "put a stout heart to a stey brae" is for you to heed on this hike, with the trail staying close to Place Creek during much of its headlong rush from its glacier to the valley floor. But there are many rewards for your exercise of stoutheartedness: magnificent falls, an adrenalin-inducing creek crossing, and sight of the glacier itself if you get that far.

As you drive north from the Mount Currie T-junction towards D'Arcy, you come to a private railway crossing on your right after 21.5 km (13.4 mi), the first of two such crossings close together. Immediately after crossing the tracks, go right on an old road that takes you south for about 600 metres to a closed gate on your left. This is private property, but the owner has consented to let hikers use the track that runs across it, so you should show your appreciation of his generosity by closing the gate behind you on entering and leaving and staying on the track that cuts across to a powerline right-of-way. Bear a little left on its far side, then follow a tree-lined avenue on the right for some 300 metres to an open space traversed by yet another powerline and with a stump directly in front of you.

From the stump, head straight into the forest on the taped route, an abandoned logging road, which at first rises relatively gently towards the creek.

Gradually you become aware of the rushing of water, until with dramatic suddenness you emerge on the edge of a chasm, face onto the falls and enshrouded in fine spray, refreshing on hot days, but making the track slippery. And now you go straight up with falls and rapids alternately on your right for the next 370 m (1200 ft) to reach a rockslide which you must negotiate. Thereafter for a time the grade eases to merely steep, so there is space for a few short switchbacks. But the relief is short-lived; the trail steepens as you go left around a rock spur, the creek for the time being below you. Soon, however, you arrive on top beside a perched erratic with the exotic name "Vodka Rock," a possible destination for the fainthearted or, at any rate, a place to draw breath and savour the views over the valley. Now the trail begins to sport a number of windfalls to provide a little high-stepping exercise as you ascend another 300 m (1000 ft) to the "bridge," a damp log perched precariously above the torrent.

Such a crossing is not for the lone traveller; in fact, a handline would be a distinct advantage, suggesting a minimum of three to a party. Here you are at about 1372 m (4500 ft), still 185 m (600 ft) below treeline, but now the grade eases, with the trail swinging away from the creek before turning back to it, the sound of more falls in your ears as you approach it again. Now you go left to cross the dam that holds back the pent-up meltwater from the glacier, and to end, if you wish, by the A-frames used by glaciologists of Canada's Geological Survey. And from here you may look westward to the sculptured peaks around Birkenhead River as you relax at last.

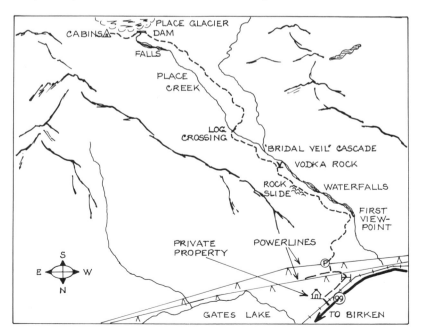

PEMBERTON

46 JOFFRE LAKES

Round trip (to upper lake)
  11 km (7 mi)
Allow 6 hours
High point 1585 (5200 ft)
Elevation gain 366 m (1200 ft)
Best July to October
Map Duffey Lake 92J/8

With three beautiful lakes en route, each lovelier than the last, and with a spectacular glacier for your destination, this hike has something for almost everyone. The road from Mount Currie, though rising steeply from the valley near the north end of Lillooet Lake to 1220 m (4000 ft), is now surfaced and should present no difficulties. However, be prepared to encounter logging trucks on working days.

Approaching Pemberton from the south, at the T-junction take the right fork for Mount Currie. At that settlement, go right again on the road to Duffy Lake and Lillooet. This takes you over Lilwat Indian land along the bank of Lillooet River, with a crossing to its north side just before the lake. Here, begin the climb to a BC Parks recreation site 23 km (14.3 mi) beyond Mount Currie and not far beyond the bridge over Joffre Creek.

The trail begins from the parking lot, heading into the trees and forking right just before the first lake on the Joffre Alpine Trail. Almost right away you have a spectacular view of the glacier from across the beautiful lake as you follow the improved trail over the marshy ground. Next comes the creek crossing, after which you start to rise, following the west side of the lake and then the creek, the sound of rushing water in your ears. Then you drop a little to a rock slide, followed by quite a steep stretch before you cross the

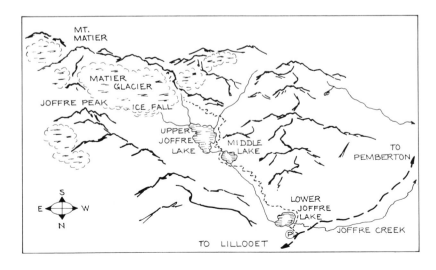

Glacier above Upper Joffre Lake

creek once more just before the second lovely body of water, the unimaginatively named Middle Lake. Work around this to the left and over the stream again, then drop briefly to its shore before continuing uphill.

Finally comes the jewel of the three lakes, nestling beneath the lowering icefalls from Matier Glacier. The trail itself heads to the right above the shoreline, then rises over talus, finally becoming a cairned route as it veers east across the creek and ends just below the snout of the glacier. In addition to the superb views of the lake and the surrounding country, with its stark evidence of recent glaciation, there is the special thrill of crashing ice blocks on a warm afternoon.

47 BLOWDOWN CREEK

Round trip (to pass) 13 km (8 mi)
Allow 5 hours
High point 2195 m (7200 ft)
Elevation gain 580 m (1900 ft)
Best July to September
Map Duffey Lake 92J/8

If you are making the trip from Pemberton to Lillooet by Duffey Lake, why not take the chance to break your journey? Stretch your legs by ascending to the pass that leads into the scenic valley of Cottonwood Creek (a tributary of the Stein River), or if you prefer a leisurely outing, stop at the very beautiful lake that nestles below it on its west side.

After its steep climb up Joffre Creek from Mount Currie, the road levels off, then starts a gentle descent along the valley of Cayoosh Creek to Duffey Lake, running along its east side. From the Forest Service Recreation Site near the end of the lake, Blowdown Creek is just over 2 km (1.2 mi) north, and the road, cutting back sharp right, is 1.5 km (0.9 mi) beyond that. It is not marked. On it you may drive without too much difficulty (except perhaps for a short hill near the end) for 10 km (6.2 mi) to a large open space on the left. Beyond this point a private mining road, recently rerouted, heads for the pass, but it has already suffered from avalanches and wash-outs and is hardly to be recommended for the average vehicle. As you follow it up the valley, you reach the point where the new road doubles back on an S-bend, while the old, now disused and trail-like, goes straight on. For hikers, the old is preferable, especially as it provides an approach to the lake already mentioned.

If you wish to make the lake your destination, drop off to the right, heading for the meadow near its outlet. Otherwise, by staying with the road you come to the pass and look into a beautiful U-shaped valley plentifully bedecked with heather and alpine flowers in the short summer season. The road itself goes as far as Silver Queen Mine, beyond which an old pack trail, now overgrown and obscure in places, continues downstream along the South Fork to its junction with the North Fork of Cottonwood Creek, and eventually links with the main improved trail down the Stein River to its mouth.

If you decide to spend a day or so in the area, you have no lack of camping spots on either side of the pass. From here you may explore ridges north and south of the pass, head over to the valley of the North Cottonwood, or ascend Gott Peak, which stands sentinel to the north of the divide. The country is all open and the views seem to go on forever.

Gott Peak, incidentally, commemorates a noted Indian fugitive who eluded the Mounties for several years. Another comment: the area supports a number of grizzlies; be careful, therefore, when hiking or camping, especially with food supplies.

View south from the old mine road

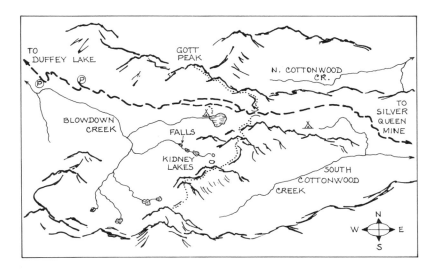

North over Tundra Lake

PEMBERTON

48 LIZZIE CREEK

Round trip (to cabin) 5 km (3 mi)
Allow 3 hours
High point 1585 m (5200 ft)
Elevation gain 260 m (850 ft)
Best July to September
Map Stein Lake 92J/1

If you are in the Pemberton area, you may make this an outing to Lizzie Creek cabin. It also provides a fine backpacking approach to the scenic alpine country that stretches over the divide towards Stein Lake, an unspoiled region of great natural beauty. Even the drive in is delightful—most of it, anyway. In Mount Currie, go right on the Duffey Lake Road to Lillooet, pass the Lilwat Indian Band's information booth, then at 10.1 km (6.3 mi), a little beyond the head of Lillooet Lake, fork right on the Pemberton-Douglas Forest Road with its warning of no gas stations for 200 km. Following the lake's east shore, you pass Lizzie Bay Recreation Site on your right after 15.4 km (9.6 mi), then head left some 600 metres beyond where a painted sign on a rock indicates your turnoff, just after you have crossed a creek.

Your road has Lizzie Creek on its right as you ascend the valley, rising gently for 8 km (5 mi). Then comes a dramatic change as you swing steeply uphill, ignoring a right fork (unless you want to make a short sidetrip to a waterfall). At the next fork you go right, but the road now becomes rough, steep and narrow, and a 4WD vehicle is recommended for the final 2 km (1.2 mi), towards the end of which you turn into the upper valley and the parking area beside Lizzie Lake, a distance of 11 km (6.8 mi) from the road along Lillooet Lake.

From Lizzie Lake the trail rises steeply for about 30 minutes, before bringing you into a narrow gorge with the romantic local name, The Gates of Shangri-La. Beyond this, after a scramble over a large rock slide, you arrive at a small mountain cabin. This is open to the public, so treat it tenderly in order that others may benefit from the generosity of its builders. Here the trail ends, but you are now in open meadows; with more than one day at your disposal you may visit as many lakes as you can possibly desire.

A full day's round trip from here brings you to a view over the most beautiful of the lakes—Tundra Lake—just over the Stein Divide, its deep blue waters catching every trick of sun's rays. Closer at hand, though, are bodies of water almost as attractive: Arrowhead Lakes, Iceberg Lake, London and Sapphire, for instance. For the ridge walker, there is Famine Ridge to the south, with the aptly named Cloudraker Mountain rising high above. For sheer delight, this area is hard to beat.

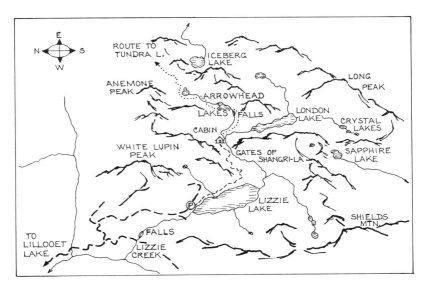

FRASER VALLEY NORTH

49 DIEZ VISTAS TRAIL

Round trip 17 km (10.5 mi)
Allow 6 hours
High point 607 m (1990 ft)
Elevation gain 455 m (1490 ft)
Best April to November
Map Coquitlam 92G/7

Whatever one thinks of B.C. Hydro in general, that corporation must be given full credit for its combination of water storage with recreation in the area surrounding Buntzen Lake, where hiking, horseback riding and water recreation may be enjoyed. And, in the case of this trail, building of a floating bridge over the south arm of the lake makes possible a delightful trip, half of it on Buntzen Ridge itself, the rest along the lake.

To reach your starting point, turn left on Ioco Drive off Highway 7A at the traffic light just east of Port Moody. Thereafter, follow signs for Anmore, the village just outside the recreation area. Having passed Anmore General Store, you drive right on a gravel road to the parking area by South Beach, going as far west as possible. From here, walk back south to the end of the lot to pick up your route, an old logging road which you soon leave, branching right for the crossing of the lake arm. The trail, common to both horse riders and hikers here, starts on the opposite side of the road that you find yourself on. Heading uphill in forest, you come to a fork in about 20 minutes, and here the foot-trail, marked with a large orange square and signed "Diez Vistas," goes off left. In another 20 minutes you break into the open at a saddle that carries an old pipeline and powerline at right angles to your line of travel, as you realize when the markers take you under the pipe and onto a trail that switchbacks upward. Near the top of a steep section, the trail forks, either branch having its own reward, the left a viewpoint over

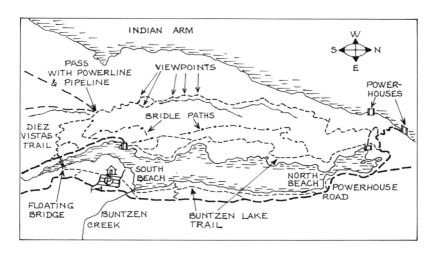

Looking up Indian Arm

Indian Arm, the right a fine outlook across South Beach to Eagle Ridge, before reuniting at the high point.

Now you travel north in open forest with, from time to time, some sensational views over Indian Arm, its waters appearing to be directly below you. The traverse of the ridge takes some 90 minutes, after which you drop fairly steeply on an old road, at the end of which you come on Hydro's service road around the lake. On it you go right, eventually reaching the lake's northern arm and, at right angles to your line of travel, trails going right and left.

Left here is the long way around, via the lake's east side, so right it is, along the powerline first of all, with striking views across to Swan Falls. And you stay with the powerline until, just after a high point, the trail swings sharp right into the forest to avoid a bushy descent into a bay. Now you remain in trees for about 30 minutes, eventually arriving below a height of land with yet another choice: over the top or around by the lakeshore. Whichever you choose, the trails rejoin near a pumphouse, and you are on the road that leads to your original crossing on the footbridge for what should have been a stimulating and energetic outing.

50 LINDSAY LAKE

Round trip 14 km (8.8 mi)
Allow 6 hours
High point 1144 m (3750 ft)
Elevation gain 960 m (3150 ft)
Best June to October
Map Coquitlam 92G/7

Not content with creating the trail along Buntzen Ridge, the indefatigable Halvor Lunden has produced no fewer than three access routes to Eagle Ridge on the opposite side of the valley. These are designed, too, so that they may serve as outings in their own right or, for organized parties, as parts of a ridge traverse from south to north or vice versa.

Of these, the most southerly has Lindsay Lake as its designated destination, the route passing Eagle Mountain on the west side—not the true high point of the ridge, it should be noted—and parking again is in the area that serves Buntzen Lake's south beach, but this time you head back to the gate on Powerhouse Road. From it, walk 20 metres north, then go right and then left onto a horse trail under a powerline. Thereafter, you turn right on a taped route and start climbing the ridge's steep west side until, beyond the Polytrichum Lookout, you round the head of the gully, a tricky little section, before you emerge from trees onto the lunar landscape typical of recent logging operations.

Such exposure is mercifully brief and soon you are beyond the limits of present logging as you walk briefly along an old dyke, part of a system once

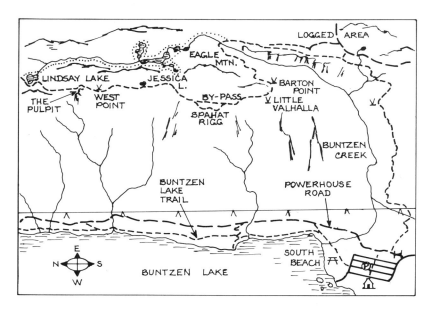

Mount Seymour under cloud, Runner, Elsay and Bishop from "Polytrichum Lookout"

used to divert waters from the plateau lakes into Noons Creek. Next the trail crosses a creek and swings southward, signs of human activity now minimal except for Halvor's lookouts, each one named, so that you pass in succession Barton Point, Little Valhalla and, as you turn north again, by way of a detour left, Spahat Rigg (Bear Ridge).

Still heading north, you come on the interesting little Jessica Lake, its waters contained within natural dykes and actually above the level of its surroundings. Its drainage is presumably subterranean, for there is no sign of an outflow channel. Thereafter, having circled Eagle Mountain, you reach another overlook, West Point, near a rocky outcrop aptly named The Pulpit, then, following a short, steep rise, you descend gently to the lake that is your objective. Of course, you could make any of the viewpoints your destination, with the possibility of using the Spahat Rigg Bypass on your return trip.

To vary your return trip, you may follow the trail round to the lake's north end, then branch off right on a taped route, which takes you across the outlet to the creek's west side and down by several small lakes, passing between the last two to recross to the east side before rejoining your outward trail at the dyke.

Across Coquitlam Lake to Coquitlam Mountain and Golden Ears

FRASER VALLEY NORTH

51 EAGLE PEAK

Round trip 17.7 km (11 mi)
Allow 8 hours
High point 1266 m (4150 ft)
Elevation gain 1083 m (3550 ft)
Best July to October
Map Coquitlam 92G/7

This feature, the true summit of Eagle Ridge, may be attained by hiking the length of Buntzen Lake to a little beyond North Beach, the corollary being that you have to retrace your steps along the lake at the end of the day if you have not gone for the ridge traverse south to Buntzen Creek. Once more, the South Beach parking lot is your point of departure. This time, however, you drop towards the beach, then go right to cross Buntzen Creek just above the point where it enters the lake.

The trail system along the east shore, even though it is a little more upsy-downsy, obviates the need to trudge along Powerhouse Road. When you do emerge on the road, a short distance short of North Beach, you may note the intake tunnel that carries water from Coquitlam Lake in the next valley to the east. In any event, you press on, passing North Beach and crossing the wide Trout Creek, whose unofficially named Swan Falls, high above, you are soon going to view from close quarters.

Just after the creek, you turn back sharp right where the road approaches the Hydro powerline, and make for pylon 531.3, a little before which your trail strikes off left, making for the trees. Now comes the relentless slog up the steep track, with the creek on your right. After some 30 minutes, however, comes temporary relief: a short spur to the right gives you a grandstand view over the lake from the top of the lower fall.

You have yet one more excuse for a rest, some fifteen minutes later, on a bluff high above the creek, from which lofty perch you look across Buntzen Ridge to the mountains of the North Shore and south over the Fraser lowlands. On resuming, you continue to rise before side-hilling into the upper basin, crossing two small tributaries (sometimes dry) en route. Now comes an enormous wash-out where the loss of vegetative cover encourages slippage and where you need to keep in view the trail markers on the opposite side. Some 20 minutes later you enter a surprisingly extensive meadow, green and lush but, unfortunately, home also to a good many flies, so you want to reach the col as quickly as you can. Here you meet the ridge trail, on which you turn right for Eagle Peak, where you have fine but slightly restricted views, the best being found at the triangulation marker on a bare bluff a little south and lower than the peak. The nearly panoramic outlook encompasses the mountains to the northeast, Mount Baker across the Fraser Valley, the Strait of Georgia beyond Vancouver and its waterways, and down below on one side Coquitlam Lake, and on the other Indian Arm.

For your return you must decide between retracing your outward steps or continuing south along the ridge to join the trail to Lindsay Lake (Hike 50). There is little difference in total distance.

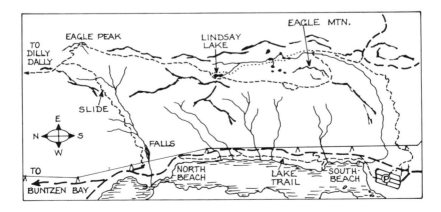

FRASER VALLEY NORTH

52 DILLY-DALLY TRAIL

Round trip 25.5 km (16 mi)
Allow 10 hours
High point 1250 m (4100 ft)
Elevation gain 1190 m (3900 ft)
Best July to October
Map Coquitlam 92G/7

You won't find Dilly-Dally Peak on any map; it is, however, the name given to a point on north Eagle Ridge, because to get there and back in one day, you can't afford to dilly-dally on the way. Actually, this outing gives the choice of two objectives, the one just mentioned and, for a shorter, less strenuous, hike, a bluff overlooking Indian Arm and giving unsurpassed views of that body of water as well as of the whole ridge on its west side from Mount Seymour north to Mount Bishop.

Like the trip to Eagle Peak, the approach to this objective involves a walk along the east side of Buntzen Lake, but after the former route goes off right, you continue on the Hydro service road past the dam with its tunnel to the powerhouse overlooking Indian Arm. A short distance beyond, the road forks, and you stay right and uphill, heading for the tiny settlement of Buntzen Bay. Before then, however, you branch off right again on a dead-end that leads to a power pylon, beyond which a trail heads off uphill to the trees above the right-of-way.

Next you turn left, cross two small creeks in an area once logged over, and join the one-time logging access road as that starts its steep ascent. Now you quickly gain height—being careful not to slip when the wooden surface is damp—and after a little more than two hours from your setting out, you reach a left fork that leads you to Crocker Lookout with its fine overlook of Indian Arm, a satisfying destination for a short day.

The next viewpoint is on the right as you work back south, and soon thereafter you reach the end of the old road and the limits of logging. Now a taped route leads you up through pleasant open forest to the main ridge,

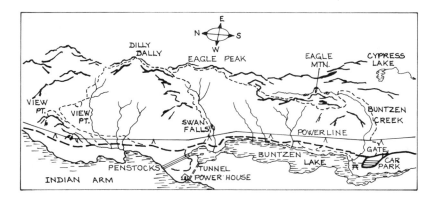

Part of the old logging road—*H. Lunden*

reaching it at a pass some 1040 m (3400 ft) in height. For the summit, however, you must still gain over 200 m (650 ft) before your dalliance can begin,
with two lakes, one east, one west below you, and mountains all around.

But you are still far from your point of departure, so here again you have
to decide whether to retrace your steps or travel south to the Eagle Peak
Trail with its steep descent via Swan Falls (Hike 51). And, of course, if you
are fit and ambitious, you may traverse the whole ridge, descending by the
trail described in Hike 50.

Coquitlam Mountain from Burke Ridge

FRASER VALLEY NORTH

53 BURKE RIDGE

Round trip (road and ridge)
20 km (12.5 mi)
Allow 8 hours
High point 1220 m (4000 ft)
Elevation gain 854 m (2800 ft)

Round trip (lakes loop)
12 km (7.5 mi)
Allow 6 hours
High point 960 m (3150 ft)
Elevation gain 860 m (2825 ft)
Best May to October
Map Coquitlam 92G/7

Although this close-in subalpine area has been designated as a park for a number of years, it remains undeveloped, and access continues to be a problem for the ordinary car owner. Perhaps, then, you should have an alternative in mind if you should find yourself with a long, dreary road to hike before you ever reach the ridge with its trail.

Travel on Highway 7 east through Port Coquitlam, then go left on Coast Meridian Road. Follow this north for some 5 km (3 mi) before turning right on Harper Road. Stay right at the Gun Club turnoff and continue for another 500 metres or so to where the road bends sharp left. Here you may park if the road is impassable and you wish to continue on foot. In any event, continue for some 3.5 km (2 mi) to a fork at Tower Hill, where the right branch is signposted Munro Lake. Take the left fork here; it leads to the few remains of the one-time ski chalet. Just north, the trail leads half right into the bush and turns up the far side of a small creek.

This trail, rough at first, improves as it proceeds past a number of small lakes, pools fringed with evergreens, and stretches of heathery meadows. At its north end, the ridge drops away before sweeping upward towards Widgeon Peak; to the left stands Coquitlam Mountain, and over to the northeast Mount Judge Howay and Robie Reid are dominant.

But what will be the alternative should you be discouraged by the long approach? Well, you can explore the lower east side of the ridge by leaving Coast Meridian on Apel Drive, which turns into Victoria. Hereafter, follow the signs to Minnekhada Regional Park as your road loses its surface and becomes Quarry Road. Having passed the entrance to Minnekhada, drive another 3.1 km (1.9 mi) to where your route starts on the left, signposted Burke Mountain Park.

Beginning on an old logging road, you soon turn right on a path marked with large red diamonds. After rising steeply for some 45 minutes, the track levels off before it is joined from the left by the ski village trail, marked with yellow. The trail here is wet in places as you approach what is left of Munro Lake now that its dam has been removed.

If you are not afraid of boggy going and a little bush, you may continue around the lake's west side to where tapes mark the stepping stones across an inlet creek. Just beyond, more tapes head off left and uphill on an old trail, now overgrown in spots, to Dennett Lake, some 120 m (400 ft) above, a rampart of cliffs behind it.

From here, another swampy route (with blue diamonds) leads southward to connect with the yellow trail on which you turn left to return to your original trail for your descent, enlivened by occasional glimpses over the Pitt River lowlands to the Fraser Valley beyond.

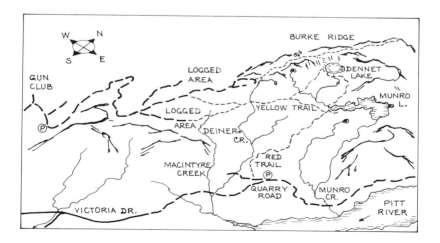

119

FRASER VALLEY NORTH

54 WIDGEON LAKE

Round trip 18.5 km (11.7 mi)
Allow 9 hours
High point 760 m (2500 ft)
Best June to September
Map Coquitlam 92G/7

Here is another trail with an interesting approach: by canoe across Pitt River. This does, though, add over two hours to the length of your day, so an early start is essential if you are to enjoy a little time at this scenic body of water, which is hemmed in by granite bluffs except at its outlet to the west fork of Widgeon Creek.

Driving east on the Lougheed Highway, go left on the Dewdney Trunk Road shortly after crossing the Pitt River. Stay on Dewdney Trunk for about 6.2 km (4 mi), then turn left on 208 Street (Neaves Road). This later becomes Rannie Road as it travels north to the public launching ramp just before Pitt Lake, nearly 18 km (11.25 mi) from the Pitt River bridge.

After donning your life jacket, paddle across the river to the north end of Siwash Island, where you enter Widgeon Slough. After 800 metres, keep right and start ascending Widgeon Creek. Stay with the main channel, going left, then right, to reach the landing place after another 3 km (2 mi) and about an hour's paddle altogether from the ramp at Rannie Road end. From here you travel on foot, taking a gravel logging road that parallels the south

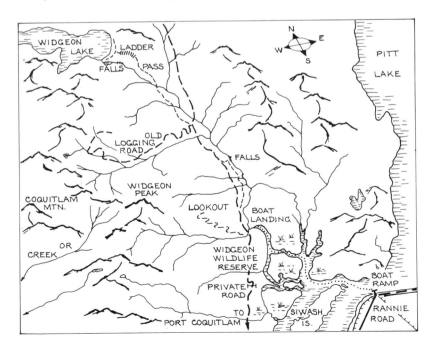

Widgeon Valley from the Pitt River dyke – *G. J. Harris*

side of the creek. You may, however, follow a foot-trail closer to the creek that leads you to some falls before rejoining the road.

The one major point of decision comes after about 4 km (2.5 mi), where you go left instead of crossing Widgeon Creek. Finally you do cross the creek's west fork and climb quite steeply to the end of the old road and the start of the trail proper, going first through slash and then continuing in forest. Following that comes a wooden ladder designed to help you over a rock bluff, and here is your lake.

If you stay right, you finish by its shore; go left and you find yourself at its outlet, having passed, of all things, a helicopter pad en route. Either choice makes a satisfying destination. Don't forget, though, to allow time for the canoe trip once your return hike is over.

FRASER VALLEY NORTH

55 UBC RESEARCH FOREST

Round trip 15.5 km (9.7 mi)
Allow 6 hours
High point 685 m (2250 ft)
Elevation gain 610 m (2000 ft)
Best April to October
Map Coquitlam 92/G7

A pleasant feature of walking in the forest is its low altitude, making it good for winter and spring outings when higher areas may be unsuitable for tramping. In fact, some of your finest views across to Golden Ears are to be had after the first snowfalls have clothed the mountain in white. Of course, you have certain restrictions made necessary by the various research projects connected with the forest sciences; these you may find listed when you register at the entrance gate.

To reach that point, turn left off the Lougheed Highway in Haney, following the signs for Golden Ears Provincial Park until you are going north on 232nd Street. Stay on this until, beyond its crossing of the North Alouette River, you turn right on Silver Valley Road (signposted); stay on it for almost 1.5 km (1 mi) to the parking lot.

In the forest several possibilities present themselves. Apart from the various short circular walks (indicated by different colour codes) around the demonstration forest, you may make a lengthy 23-km (14.5 mi) trip by Marion and Katherine lakes, following Road K on the way out and returning via H and F by Eunice and Gwendoline Lakes.

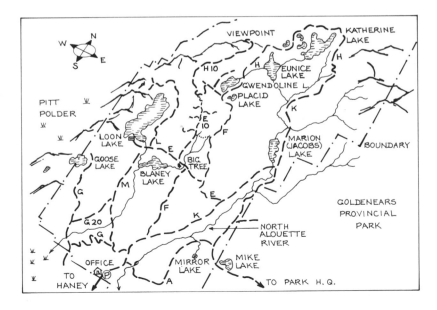

Restored donkey near the entrance

Another worthwhile hike takes you north on Road F, right at its junction with E, and left again, following F once more until you reach Placid Lake and the junction with Road H. Take H and work to the west around the lake before resuming your northerly direction towards Gwendoline Lake. Just before this body of water, leave the main road, going left and then left again on H1O, making a long swing south and back again. Stay with H1O to its end, ignoring turnoffs, as you rise steadily to a final little knoll at 685 m (2250 ft) with eye-filling prospects to the north over Pitt Lake and its surrounding peaks.

For a round trip, retrace your steps to the beginning of the S-bend just southwest of Gwendoline Lake. Here you pick up an old road, a little overgrown, going off to the right. This drops downhill south to E1O, which you follow back to E. Go left, travel east past the "Big Tree" to the junction with F and so back to your starting point. If you are keen for more exercise, you may continue east to the intersection of E and K before making your right turn.

Clouds swirling around Blanshard Needle

FRASER VALLEY NORTH

56 ALOUETTE MOUNTAIN

Round trip 21 km (13 mi)
Allow 9 hours
High point 1348 m (4421 ft)
Elevation gain 1100 m (3600 ft)
Best July to October
Map Stave Lake 92G/8

Now that Golden Ears Park exists in its own right instead of being a neglected segment of Garibaldi Provincial Park, its staff has put considerable effort into improving trails and repairing damage wrought by logging and by Hurricane Frieda, the great storm of 1962. Among routes altered both physically and aesthetically is the one that leads north from near Mike Lake to Alouette Mountain and, for climbers, to Blanshard Needle.

Travelling east on Highway 7 through Haney, turn left on 228th Street at the Golden Ears Park sign, then swing right on Dewdney Trunk Road. Go left again on 232nd, cross the South Alouette River, then travel right on Fern Crescent past Maple Ridge park into the ornamented entrance of Golden Ears Park. From here, drive 4.5 km (2.7 mi), turning off left at the

Park Headquarters sign. Go left again where the road forks and drive for just over 1.6 km (1 mi) to the signpost pointing to Incline Trail. Limited parking space is available at the trail; there is more at Mike Lake, about 300 metres along.

Incline Trail goes north, passing an interesting piece of drowned forest, then following an old logging railway grade for some distance. The route then rises to meet a logging road in about 30 minutes, shortly after passing the upper end of Eric Dunning Trail on the right. At the road, go right for some distance, then take the signposted cut-off trail uphill through second-growth timber. This trail again intersects the road, stays briefly with it, then cuts off uphill once more, finally emerging at the road again below the logged-off area that is a relic of the storm.

Cross the road and continue through prime forest northward, passing a signed trail to Lake Beautiful on the left (it's pretty but hardly justifies the title). The main trail stays west of the ridge crest, finally emerging on picturesque little subalpine meadows dotted with lakes, the objective now ahead of you. Finally comes the summit cairn with its commemorative marker and its magnificent panorama of Blanshard and Edge, Mounts Judge Howay and Robie Reid to the northeast, Pitt Lake to the west beyond UBC Forest, with Burke Ridge behind. South is the lower Fraser Valley, its horizon dominated by Mount Baker.

Although this trail is quite lengthy, it is well graded and its woodland stretches give pleasant walking on sunny days; in fact, it is interesting to contrast the second-growth timber of the lower stretches with the original tree cover at higher elevations, some of the latter being of impressive dimensions and of venerable age. Pay a visit to Mike Lake, too, when you are in the area; it's an attractive body of water for a picnic.

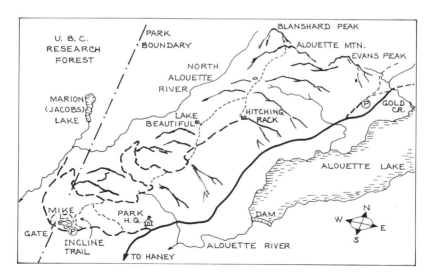

57 GOLDEN EARS

Round trip 24 km (15 mi)
Allow 10 hours or overnight
High point 1706 m (5598 ft)
Elevation gain 1500 m (4920 ft)
Best July to September
Maps Coquitlam 92G/7,
Stave Lake 92G/8

Once you have hiked the Alouette Mountain Trail, you may feel that you are ready for the peak from which this provincial park takes its name. Remember, the trail to this summit involves a strenuous long day's outing, but the magnificent views from the objective are ample compensation, coupled as they are with the sense of well-being that comes from accomplishment. However, a mountain shelter on Panorama Ridge at 1160 m (3800 ft) may be your destination if you think the longer hike is beyond you.

From the park entrance, follow the main access road past the sani-station and the information board, then fork left and left again for the hiker parking lot (the right branches lead to campgrounds and the day-use area). From here, follow the signs from West Canyon Trail, which takes you north with Gold Creek on your right. En route, you find Evans Creek and enjoy a variety of valley scenes, culminating in the outlook from a viewpoint before bearing left up the next valley. Then you cross several creeks until finally, just after the camping spot at Alder Flats, you meet an old logging road coming up from Gold Creek parallel to an east-flowing tributary.

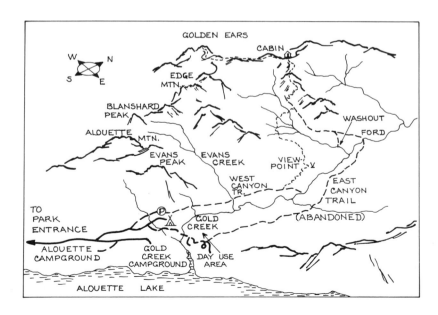

Edge Mountain from the subsidiary ridge

On this you go left, switchbacking upward for a short distance before climbing dramatically to the ridge crest at its lower end and resuming your northwesterly direction until you reach the little mountain shelter, where you change course again onto the ridge heading southwest to the summit. Your route is now adorned with a number of bumps, but with superb views of Pitt Lake and the mountains to the west as compensation. All the time you are gaining height steadily, and eventually you leave all vegetation behind as you approach and cross a permanent snowfield and turn back westward for the final stretch—one steep enough for hands to be called into service frequently as you make for the peak of the North Ear. Here you have a true panorama from your elevated perch.

For this trip, come prepared; the weather may change quickly in the mountains. Care and proper equipment are also necessary if you aim for the peak. On the other hand, you may enjoy a leisurely ridge walk, if you set your sights lower, with some toothsome blueberries to sample in season, fruit that bears may also enjoy. Mountain goats may be seen also, and though the logging whistle has long been silent on the old railway grade up Gold Creek, you may hear instead the squeak of the pika among the rocks.

58 MOUNT ST. BENEDICT

Round trip 14.5 km (9 mi)
Allow 7 hours
High point 1250 m (4100 ft)
Elevation gain 1030 m (3380 ft)
Best July to October
Map Stave Lake 92G/8

It would be appropriate if the name of this peak has some connection with the Benedictine Community in Mission. One of its members, the late Fr. Damasus Payne, was an ardent climber who loved the mountains for the sense they gave him of the presence of God. On this mountain, with its magnificent views that cry out for photography, it is easy to share his feeling.

To reach the start of this hike, travel east from Mission City on Highway 7 for just over 6.4 km (4 mi) and turn off sharp left on Sylvester Road immediately before a small country store. Drive north, at first over blacktop on the valley floor but later rising steadily on a gravel road. Some 17 km (10.6 mi) from your turnoff, you leave your vehicle in a small parking lot just north of Murdo Creek in Davis Lake Provincial Park. Now walk back south across the bridge over the creek and look for the trail leading uphill eastward, the stream being below you on your left.

At first you ascend through open forest, then—still above the creek—you meet a logging road on which you walk left. Almost immediately, however, you go left again on an older, badly washed-out road. Stay with this while gaining altitude, veering to the right as you reach the upper valley, finally heading in a southerly direction as you approach its head. Now a trail with orange markers leads you through new-growth timber over a poorly drained stretch towards a prominent buttress, near the foot of which nestles

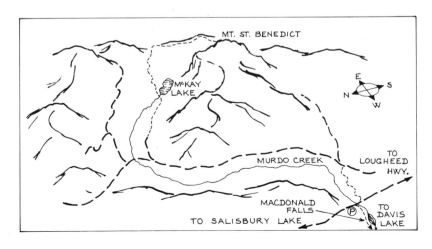

Glimpse of Judge Howay from the ridge

McKay Lake, about 4 km (2.5 mi) from your starting point. Skirt the lake on the left and make for the ridge above.

Once you have reached the col above the lake, your trail goes to the right, ascending the ridge and gradually turning north and west to your destination. Here is a summit that, on a fine day, you will be in no hurry to leave, and you may well feel like echoing Fr. Payne's pious remark, "We expressed sincere thanks to Almighty God for the splendour of His Creation." That splendour is reflected in the waters of the lake below and from the snowy slopes of Judge Howay and Robie Reid as these peaks brood majestically over the scene.

59 BEAR MOUNTAIN

Round trip 19 km (12 mi)
Allow 6 hours
High point 1040 m (3400 ft)
Elevation gain 1005 m (3300 ft)
Best June to October
Map Harrison Lake 92H/5

This mountain block overlooks Harrison Lake from the east and is guaranteed to give a day of not too strenuous exercise, with some striking views over the Fraser valley to top it off. You may end the hike with a visit to the pool at the hot springs to rid yourself of any aches and pains suffered in the ascent. For a start, though, drive north from Agassiz on Highway 9, heading for Harrison Hot Springs.

In the village, turn right on Lillooet Avenue one block south of the lake and follow it and its continuation, Rockwell Drive, for 4.9 km (3.1 mi) north around Crowhurst Bay, passing en route an arts centre and Rivtow marine depot. Finally, near the top of a hill, a rough road forks off right, a property on either side. The road soon deteriorates, so use the wide area at its beginning for parking. As you walk up the road, you are soon confronted by a gate and a fence announcing the private property of Kerr Addison Mines, so you go right on the old road, staying outside the fence.

Now you stay with the travelled logging road as it heads mainly south. At the first main fork go right, then switchback upward, passing a pretty little waterfall. At the next fork, go left and start a long traverse north on bare talus slopes that provide spectacular views of Harrison Lake directly below you. As you near the ridge, the road swings again, and once more you fork right then stay left just before a lake, which you pass on the east.

Black bear grazing

View up Harrison Lake from the logging road

One more right fork and you continue south on a somewhat overgrown old logging road that eventually swings back to the west side of the ridge. Ignore all left forks until, almost at the end of the road system in a little draw, you head half left uphill to the standing timber on an even older road that gives way to a marked route. This soon brings you to your destination as you burst into the open close to a triangulation point. The mighty peaks of the Cheam group face you from across the Fraser, contrasting with the puny evidences of human activity on the valley floor.

Note: The old road beyond the lake has become so very overgrown that it is no longer recommended.

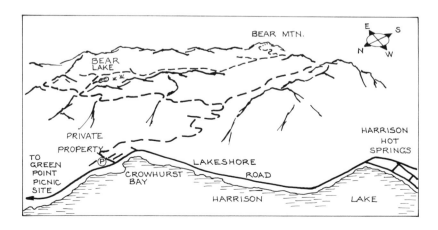

HARRISON LAKE

60 LOOKOUT PEAK

Round trip 18 km (11 mi)
Allow 6 hours
High point 1530 m (5020 ft)
Elevation gain 860 m (2800 ft)
Best July to October
Map Harrison Lake 92H/5

This trip gives unparalleled views of Harrison Lake from its east side, the route taking you north, rising to just over 1500 m (5000 ft) from a start point near sea level at Harrison Hot Springs.

As with the approach to Bear Mountain, you travel north from Harrison Hot Springs, following the sign for Sasquatch Provincial Park. Where a road goes left to a picnic site and another branches right for Deer Lake and Hicks Lake, continue straight ahead, finally reaching the beginning of Harrison Lake East Logging Road 1.1 km (0.7 mi) beyond the park entrance. Travel along Harrison Lake East for 4.8 km (3 mi) to an old road cutting back sharp right and uphill. On it, drive back south for 1.85 km (1 mi) to turn sharp left on an even older road that first winds steeply upward, then levels off. This you follow 3.4 km (2.1 mi) from the last intersection to an old landing area high above Harrison Lake near a rocky shoulder.

From here you travel on foot, using an old washed-out road, overgrown in places. After about 1.6 km (1 mi), fork left and make your way across Slollicum Creek as best you can, then continue north on the creek's west side, gradually rising along a ridge that parallels the lake. Finally with an S-bend you reach the ridge that points to your objective, a bare knoll about 800 metres beyond the end of the old logging track that you have been following.

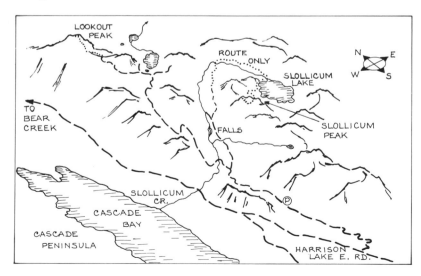

132

Across the Fraser Valley to the Cheam Range — *W. Cadillac*

There is no longer a visible trail, so to reach the peak descend slightly into a shallow hollow, work through the new growth in the logged-off area and head north up the ridge through standing timber. From the summit there are fine views up and down Harrison Lake, while mountain vistas range from Old Settler in the northeast to Mount Baker, which dominates the southwestern skyline.

As an alternative, stay right at the fork before Slollicum Creek. By so doing, you follow the creek on its right side, past its falls. Cross the creek and continue on its east side to the lake and basin northeast of Slollicum Peak. This peak is another possible destination for experienced hikers in organized groups who are not scared off by the "terrible supernatural being," the meaning of Slollicum in Halkomelem, the language of the Chehalis Indians.

Note: The "old washed-out road" has recently been improved to facilitate forest replanting and maintenance, so that it is now possible, given a suitable vehicle, to drive as far as Slollicum Creek, about 2 km (1.2 mi) beyond and 200 m (650 ft) higher than the original starting point.

FRASER VALLEY SOUTH

61 SUMAS MOUNTAIN

Round trip (from west)
   13.5 km (8.5 mi)
Allow 6 hours
High point 885 m (2900 ft)
Elevation gain 715 m (2350 ft)

Round trip (from east) 21 km (13 mi)
Allow 8 hours
Elevation gain 870 m (2850 ft)
Best May to November
Map Sumas 92G/1

Those who like doing things the easy way may simply follow the Sumas Mountain Park signs from the Highway 1 turnoff 15.4 km (9.5 mi) east of the Mission-Sumas Exit at Abbotsford. These point the way north on Sumas Mountain Road for 7.8 km (4.8 mi) to a right turn on Batt Road for the park. More strenuous hikes, using the B.C. Centennial Trail as approaches, are possible, however, from both west and east. You may thus go to the summit and return to your original starting point or, with a two-car party, turn the outing into a crossover.

For the western approach, stay on Sumas Mountain Road for 1.7 km (1 mi) beyond Batt Road to find orange markers on the right of a bend as you descend steeply to the north. From the road, drop over the bank to an old road below and go right to cross a creek, then leave the road again, following the orange markers carefully to avoid straying onto the private property all around the trail. Next you descend to Wades Creek, its name indicative of what you may have to do in crossing when the water is high. Now climb out of the gully to go right on an old road for about 1 km (0.7 mi) to a tributary creek, a short distance beyond which, on a relatively flat stretch, you make an abrupt change of direction: ninety degrees and uphill once more, the orange markers now supplemented by those of the 1967 Centennial.

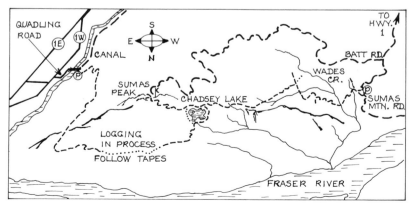

Looking up the Fraser River from the peak

The path is now much less complicated than heretofore, and you rise through pleasant open forest to emerge for a short stretch on a steep sidehill, with glimpses to the north and upriver. Then you head into another valley, encounter a fast-flowing stream complete with small rapids, and very soon thereafter come within sight of Chadsey Lake glinting through the trees. From the picnic spot by the lake, make your way right along the south shore to the east end where the trail starts to rise once more to the double summit: Main Peak with its eye-filling sight of Mount Baker, and North Peak with its splendid views of the upper Fraser Valley and the mountains to the north.

If you wish to approach from the east, drive 10 km (6 mi) beyond the Sumas Mountain Road Exit, then turn left on No. 1 Road, go left again on the main highway, westbound for a short distance, then right on Quadling Road. Follow the road as it crosses the Sumas River and park by the dam. The trail starts opposite beneath a rocky bluff.

At first it zigzags upward quite steeply, staying west of the bluff and turning eastward only when it has gained sufficient height. Thus you reach the end of the ridge where you have Vedder Canal almost below you and where also you start to swing back westward, rising gently now along the north side in a forest of hemlock and Douglas-fir. But then comes a shocking intrusion on any beautiful thoughts inspired by these magnificent trees. Logging has commenced, and the trail has been disrupted by forest roads and logging debris. Follow the markers that guide you through this area until you reach the haven of the standing trees on its west side. Eventually you work over a shoulder and reach Chadsey Lake near the east bank of its outlet. By going clockwise along the east side of the lake, you intersect the peak trail from the picnic site, and a left turn takes you to the top.

Unusual view of Mount Baker from the ridge

FRASER VALLEY SOUTH

62 VEDDER PEAK (WEST TRAIL)

Round trip (direct) 11 km (7 mi)
Allow 5 hours

Round trip (circuit) 16 km (10 mi)
Allow 6.5 hours
High point 924 m (3029 ft)
Elevation gain 865 m (2840 ft)
Best April to November
Map Sumas 92G/1

This sporting little mountain, its elevation just under 925 m (3030 ft), makes a good outing for early or late in the year when lung-opening walks tend to be scarce. From the summit, too, you have attractive views over the Fraser Valley as well as of the Cultus Lake area.

Travelling Highway 1 east from Abbotsford, fork right at the Yarrow–Cultus Lake turnoff before the bridge over the Vedder Canal. In Yarrow, go left on Central Road to Wilson Road. Turn right here, cross the railway track, and continue on Majuba Hill Road to Highland Drive. Go sharp left here and park about 250 metres along, where an old logging road cuts back to the right before veering left (east). On this road, you ignore two right forks on the bend, a private road going left, and another right fork. Beyond this are two tracks, the work of trail bikers, one before and one after a small creek. At the next fork, with its watershed warning on the left, take the right (uphill) track.

Next you come out and turn right on a relatively flat old railway grade, but relief does not last long, and soon you take the uphill left fork once more. This you stay with for some distance before going right again. Ignore the next left as you ascend, first going west, then back east. If you want an excuse to draw breath, one is provided in the view to the north, looking along Vedder Canal towards Sumas Mountain. At the end of this road, watch for tapes marking a trail on your right. Its steep grade eases off 150 m (500 ft) higher and just before a well-marked trail junction. Here you discover that you have been on West Trail, that the route from the left is Ridge Trail, and that Peak Trail is slightly right.

From here, the peak is only a short scramble away, and with its all-round views you will be in no hurry to undertake the return trip. This may be by your original route, but if you want an alternative, follow Ridge Trail from the intersection and travel east along it for about 3 km (2 mi) before forking left. A short taped route through young trees gives access to an old logging road on which you turn right. The road has been badly eroded and hence is not too pleasant after rain. Next you reach a clearing which you cross, veering slightly left to pick up the old road again. Soon you pass a marshy area on your left, and following that you complete the S-bend enclosing a micro-wave tower. Here you have some good views across the valley before continuing westward to rejoin the original route for your return.

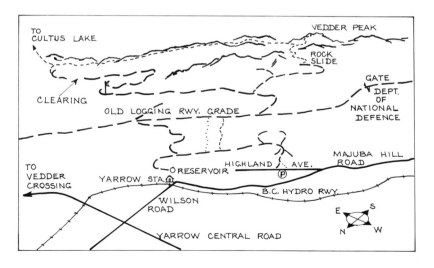

Elk Mountain meadows

63 MOUNT THURSTON

Round trip 20 km (12.5 mi)
Allow 8 hours
High point 1637 m ((5335 ft)
Elevation gain 1015 m (3330 ft)
Best July to October
Map Chilliwack 92H/4

Part of the interest of this outing is the deviousness of your approach to the parking spot, involving quite an exercise in following directions. From Highway 1 going east, beyond the Chilliwack turnoffs and just after the railway overpass, turn south (right) on Prest Road. After 4 km (2.5 mi), turn left on Bailey, and shortly thereafter take the right fork on Elk View Road as it begins to rise. Stay with the main travelled road, which twists and winds, losing its hardtop just beyond Ryder Lake Park. After nearly 10 km (6.2 mi), it becomes Chilliwack Bench Forest Road, and you park about 500 metres

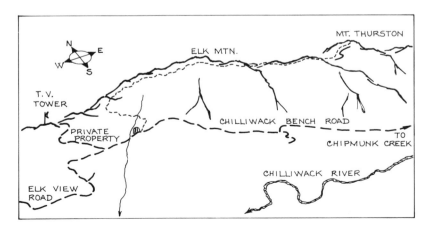

To the northeast, the slopes of Mount Mercer— *D. Ellis*

beyond in a small gravel pit on the left, the start of the trail being just a little to the south of it.

The improved trail goes behind the quarry, among trees at first, turning from northwest to east as you rise past a prominent spur. The change in direction arises from the fact that the old trail, now blocked off, began on private property. After about an hour and a half you reach the open flower meadows which should be at their best in July—as should the wild strawberries—but being dedicated hikers, you will press on, past the summit of Elk Mountain towards your objective.

On the way to your destination you have as much mountain and valley scenery as you can possibly desire. Across the Chilliwack River Valley to the south Liumchen Ridge shoulders its way upward. South and east are the Border Peaks and Mount Slesse, with snowfields on their upper reaches much of the year. North lies the valley of the Fraser, and to your left front are the peaks of the Lucky Four group. Even with strawberries to tempt you below, you will probably not wish to hurry down.

To close, two notes: Water is lacking on the ridge, so be prepared, and stay on the trails to prevent damage to fragile meadows.

FRASER VALLEY SOUTH

64 CHEAM PEAK

Round trip 31 km (19 mi)
Allow 11 hours or overnight
High point 2109 m (6913 ft)
Elevation gain 2080 m (6825 ft)
Best late July to October
Map Chilliwack 92H/4

As The Lions are to Vancouver, so Cheam is to the eastern section of the Fraser Valley, dominant over Highway 1 as it runs east from Chilliwack towards Hope. The only difficulty with this hike is its length, an optimistic estimate being 11 hours. For this reason, an overnight camp is perhaps preferable to doing the whole trip in one day. Also you should save this trip for fairly late in the summer to avoid snow and ice on the peak. The ridge, too, may be rather dry, so carry water—even though the name "Cheam" commemorates the wild strawberries that the Indians used to collect from its meadows.

After you have passed Rosedale–Agassiz turnoff, continue the short stretch to just beyond the gas station at Popkum, then turn off right on Popkum Road South. Stay left at its first fork and swing back almost to the highway before going right at a small white building marked with a trail sign. Parking space is available a little beyond, though 4WD vehicles may proceed farther up the old logging road (which is steadily deteriorating). The route, marked with red squares, poses no difficulty as you climb steadily south and west and cross Bridal Creek at 450 m (1500 ft), far above its falls in their little park.

Next, you go left at a fork and recross the creek a good deal higher as you head for a transverse ridge. At the next intersection, take the right fork as it heads first south, then gradually back north and east, rising to a view-

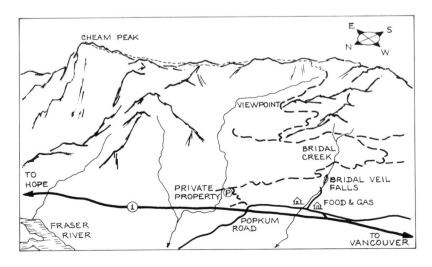

Early snow on Mount Cheam seen from Mount Laughington

point on a steep north-south ridge. Continue right from here, gradually entering a broad bowl and making for the end of the old road system.

From here, the trail proper begins, travelling generally northeast along the approach ridge to the peak some 2 hours away. It poses no technical difficulty; the only possible obstacle, a small gendarme, may be bypassed on its left as you head for the summit with its views over mountains and valleys.

A new summer route, shorter and easier than that just described, has been created recently using for access a logging road up Chipmunk Creek on the opposite (south) side of the ridge. For this approach turn left off Chilliwack Lake Road 26.9 km (16.7 mi) from Vedder Crossing, go left again at the T-junction at Foley Creek and drive 2.2 km (1.4 mi) west to a logging road, a short distance beyond the bridge over Chipmunk Creek (see Hike 68). Go right and uphill here, staying with the main logging road almost 7 km (4.3 mi) before going right on a very steep and rough road for another 4 km (2.5 mi) to the parking area beside a barrier about 1 km (.6 mi) from the trailhead at the end of the logging road. From the trailhead to the peak, the round trip is about 7.5 km (4.7 mi) with an elevation gain of 632 m (2074 ft) on a well-graded trail which, after passing little Spoon Lake, zigzags upward through the meadows towards the ridge, where, close to the peak, it joins the long trail from the Fraser Valley.

CHILLIWACK RIVER

65 MOUNT AMADIS (INTERNATIONAL RIDGE)

Round trip 16 km (10 mi)
Allow 7 hours
High point 1520 m (4995 ft)
Elevation gain 1220 m (4000 ft)

Round trip (from Edmeston Road)
    21 km (13 mi)
Allow 8 hours
Elevation gain 1400 m (4600 ft)
Best July to October
Map Chilliwack 92H/4

By what circumstance the hero of a mediaeval Spanish romance gave his name to a minor summit in B.C.'s Cascade Mountains is a mystery that you might like to ponder as you ascend International Ridge towards its high point, Mount Amadis.

To reach the start of this hike, drive through Cultus Lake village. From its Information Office travel along Columbia Valley Road for 1.3 km (0.8 mi), then go left briefly on Sleepy Hollow Road before turning off right on Vance Road. Stay on this road for the next 2.8 km (1.7 mi) to a fork, where the right, gated branch leads into a Department of National Defence training area. Go left here and at the next fork, where left leads to Liumchen Ridge, turn sharp right outside the army fence, eventually veering right and uphill. Very soon the road narrows and becomes very rough, but with a suitable

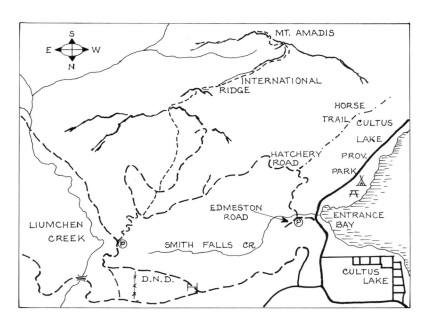

International Ridge from Liumchen Ridge: Mount Amadis centre left

vehicle you may drive the short distance to park at a clearing on the right and near another fork.

Now you follow the very eroded old road on the right as it winds steeply upward until it meets another old road (Hatchery Road, coming up from Edmeston Road) marked with an orange arrow, on which you go right, watching carefully for the markers signifying the trail on the left just below the next corner. Follow this trail as it crosses and recrosses a B.C. Land Survey Line, before emerging once more on the road. Now you go right for about 20 metres until the trail beckons you left once more, climbing steadily up the narrow ridge to a knoll.

Here you may enjoy your first uninterrupted views of Liumchen Ridge and the Chilliwack valley, though you have had glimpses en route across the Fraser valley to the north. And now the grade eases somewhat as you skirt the next summit on its east side then swing southwest towards your goal. On this stretch the ridge is wider, with occasional meadows and the sight of Mount Baker to inspire you. Finally, after dropping some 90 m (300 ft) to a saddle, you begin an ascending traverse round the treeless north side to the summit.

If logging should again disrupt the route described, you may approach from Edmeston Road by taking the Columbia Valley Road towards Cultus Lake Provincial Park and turning left near the northeast end of the lake. A fire access road with a gate across it goes right after 300 metres. Follow this road up over the nose of the ridge for just under 5 km (3 mi) to go right on the trail previously described.

CHILLIWACK RIVER

66 LIUMCHEN RIDGE

Round trip (to lake) 11 km (7 mi)
Allow 5 hours
High point 1700 m (5576 ft)
Elevation gain 480 m (1576 ft)

Round trip (to Liumchen Mountain)
  18 km (11 mi)
Allow 8 hours
High point 1830 m (6000 ft)
Elevation gain 610 m (2000 ft)
Best July to October
Map Chilliwack 92H/4

This trail is popular with hikers for the access it gives to alpine meadows along a pleasant ridge. Of interest, too, is the name (sometimes spelt "Lihumitsen"), an attempt at recording an Indian term meaning "water swirling out in gushes." No doubt this refers to the creek that at one time had a large native village near its mouth on the Chilliwack River.

Like the Mount Amadis approach (Hike 65) via Cultus Lake village and the Columbia Valley Road, this also goes left on Sleepy Hollow, then right on Vance to the fork. This time, however, you go left and left again, descending to cross Liumchen Creek and keeping right at a fork shortly after as the road begins to rise steadily. With a sturdy vehicle you may drive for about 8.5 km (5 mi) to a fork at about the 1220-m (4000-ft) level.

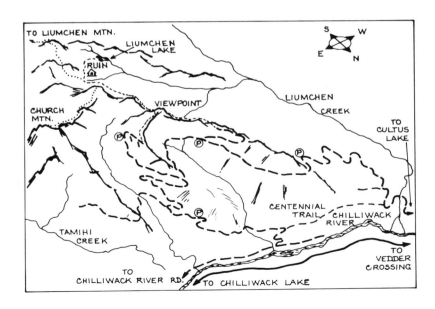

Border Peaks and Tomyhoi behind Church Mountain

After parking, follow the right fork as it rises westward, turns south and crests as it nears the trailhead. On the trail, you progress along a steep sidehill with meadows and trees until you reach the ridge proper, just south of its first high point, a possible side trip with views north across the Harrison River to the peaks around its lake, east to Slesse and the Border Peaks and southwest to Mount Baker.

The trail, well marked with orange squares, now stretches south for a good distance, keeping to the west of various minor summits, then dropping gradually into the bowl that holds Liumchen Lake. Alternatively, leaving the marked trail at a narrow, marshy meadow, you may strike up to regain the ridge at the bare summit southeast of the lake. Here a cairn suggests a possible destination, though continuing south along the ridge will eventually bring you to Liumchen Mountain itself, with its ringside views of its neighbours in the United States.

An alternative approach comes in from Chilliwack Lake Road just beyond its crossing from north bank to south about 10 km (6 mi) east of the bridge at Vedder Crossing. Turn back west here on a logging road parallel to the river and continue downstream for about 2.5 km (1.5 mi), then, having crossed a small stream, go left on a well-travelled logging road, driving as far as your vehicle permits. However you travel, continue for about 6 km (3.7 mi), heading generally southwest to a fork where you go sharp right up a steep incline for another 1.5 km (1 mi). Then you go left for 2.5 km (1.6 mi) towards the next switchback, before turning northward again to the end of the ridge. At the end of the road system an old trail heads up a fairly steep spur to meet with the trail from the west in the open meadow below the first high point.

CHILLIWACK RIVER

67 MOUNT MACFARLANE

Round trip 21 km (13 mi)
Allow 10 hours or overnight
High point 2100 m (6885 ft)
Elevation gain 1765 m (5785 ft)
Best July to September
Map Chilliwack 92H/4

Do not be put off by the somewhat alarming statistics annexed to this trip; any one of a number of intermediate points may serve as a satisying destination, notably one or other of the lakes with its surrounding meadows. The lower, Pierce Lake, lying at the end of an improved trail, has an elevation gain of 1050 m (3500 ft) and requires about 7 hours for the round trip, given that the trail rises quite steeply. Indeed, the meadows there would make an attractive destination for an easy backpacking trip and leisurely exploration of the alpine segment.

To reach the trailhead just off Chilliwack Lake Road, you must travel 22 km (13.6 mi) from Vedder Crossing, or 2.5 km (1.6 mi) after you have crossed Slesse Creek. From the turnoff, signposted for Pierce Lake, you drive some 300 metres to a Forest Service Recreation Site, where parking is provided. On foot, you start rising immediately, heading southeast in forest to cross Pierce Creek at about 975 m (3200 ft) in a stretch of particularly fine trees. Thereafter, continuing to climb, you skirt an old windfall area before gaining the level of the lake. The steepness of the valley sides forces the trail to rise above the lake before it ends in the meadows beyond the southeast corner, close to a creek from the upper basin with its unnamed lake some 305 m (1000 ft) above. This you approach by following the creek up the steep slope and switchbacking up the valley headwall, picking up an old trail at the left of the scree slope and making for the alpine meadows just

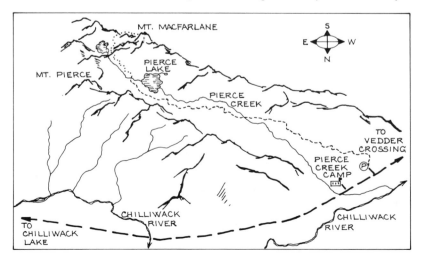

Steep slopes above Pierce Lake— *H. Lunden*

below the second lake. From here, Mount MacFarlane lies south and a little west along an open ridge, but still two hours away.

For the last stretch there is no trail, and the mountain is best approached by starting up the gully south of the peak, then swinging around to the northwest to gain the summit. Here is another panoramic viewpoint with the Border Peaks rising from the deep valley of Slesse Creek on the west and Slesse itself, 5 km (3 mi) south along the alpine ridge on which you are perched. And looking back northeast, you see Mount Pierce, much diminished from here, its summit, 140 m (460 ft) lower than yours, also attainable from the upper lake.

Beyond the end of the improved trail, this trip is for hikers who are both fit and experienced in route-finding. It is particularly important to note where to pick up the route down from the meadows north of the upper lake, so that your descent is without misadventure.

[handwritten annotation: wrong — follow ridge. Avoid North]

147

Looking south up the Nesakwatch: Slesse Mountain on the right

CHILLIWACK RIVER

68 MOUNT LAUGHINGTON

Round trip 14 km (9 mi)
Allow 6 hours
High point 1775 m (5820 ft)
Elevation gain 755 m (2470 ft)
Best July to October
Map Chilliwack 92H/4

The 1972 trail to this pleasant open ridge and summit began from an old logging road reached by turning left after crossing to the north side of Foley Creek and driving 400 metres before going sharp right. However, renewed logging activity has disrupted the trail so, for the time being, this is no longer an attractive route. Still, there are compensations, for, by using the Airplane Creek logging road to the east, with 4WD you are able to drive to about 1020 m (3350 ft) before taking to foot, enabling you to spend more time in the subalpine country below the high point.

To reach your starting point, turn left off Chilliwack Lake Road just after it has recrossed to the north side of the river, 26.9 km (16.7 mi) east of the flashing light at Vedder Crossing. Staying close to the river at first, and ignoring one fork to the right, you cross Foley Creek after 2 km (1.2 mi) and go right at the T-junction. Now drive for 2.4 km (1.5 mi), recrossing Foley Creek en route, to go left at another T-junction, crossing Foley Creek yet again. Remain on the creek's west side, switchbacking upward, ignoring one left fork after 1.7 km (1 mi) and parking at a second at about 2.5 km (1.5 mi).

On foot, take the left fork, following the road which is now rough and steep in spots. Stay right after some 40 minutes, noting that the road from the left intersects the old trail, then keep right once more after another 30 minutes and continue to the end of the road at about 1600 m (5200 ft). On this part of the trip so far, the saving grace has been the stunning views, with Williams Peak, Rexford, Slesse and McGuire prominent to the south, while the Cheam Range and Lucky Four peaks dominate to north and east.

From the end of the road, a taped route takes you through an old burned-over area to the end of the ridge proper, passing to the left of a bare knoll at about 1630 m (5300 ft)—a possible destination for a short day. Your route beyond here, ill-defined in places at first, becomes more distinct as you proceed along the main ridge, perhaps gloating a little as you contrast the ease of your ascent with the long slog faced by your predecessors using the old trail.

Two things more: on a south-facing slope, this hike can be warm in summer, so fall is a good time for the trip; and do pick a clear day to take the fullest advantage of the views.

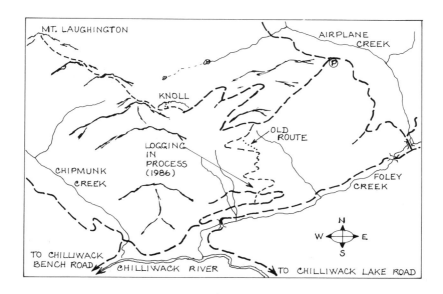

149

CHILLIWACK RIVER

69 WILLIAMSON LAKE

Round trip 13 km (8 mi)
Allow 7 hours
High point 1655 m (5430 ft)
Elevation gain 1175 m (3850 ft)
Best July to October
Map Chilliwack 92H/4

In a high cirque with the majestic peaks of the Lucky Four mountain group around it lies Williamson Lake, site of a small B.C. Mountaineering Club cabin until an avalanche swept it out of existence in 1972.

To reach the start of this hike, turn left off Chilliwack Lake Road 26.9 km (16.7 mi) from the Vedder Crossing bridge, about 100 metres after it crosses back to the north side of the river. Stay left at the first fork, then after 2 km (1.2 mi) cross Foley Creek and turn right. From here drive 4.1 km (2.5 mi), recrossing Foley Creek en route, to where orange markers on the left indicate the beginning of the trail beside a small creek and opposite a turnout where you may park (if you arrive at the Forest Service Recreation Site, you have gone too far).

The trail descends to cross the creek at the outlet from Foley Lake, where you may see the remnants of the footbridge put in by the Forest Service a few years ago. From late summer into fall, the creek bed is almost dry, so crossing should be relatively easy at those times, even without a bridge. Once across, you pick up the markers on the north side and start rising steeply, following a prominent spur of Welch Peak. Above treeline you bear right and work your way eastward along a steep sidehill, making your way

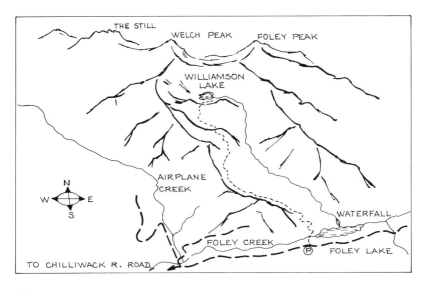

Mounts Welch and Foley stand guard above Williamson Lake – *D. Ellis*

ever upward to the high basin in which your objective is located. The towering peaks of Welch, Foley and The Still provide a noble background. The scene is austere and awe-inspiring: a setting for exalted thoughts, not everyday trifles.

Note that this is not a hike for spring or early summer, there being definite avalanche danger at higher elevations; and down below there is the lake outlet to contend with—no easy matter at high water.

Given the possible difficulty of crossing the creek, you may try the following alternative, though it does involve a short bushwhack. Backtrack 1.6 km (1 mi) to Airplane Creek logging road, cross the bridge there, and go right just beyond. The road you are now on takes you over Airplane Creek, then rises steeply as it heads east. From its farthest point in that direction, contour in open forest to intersect the trail.

CHILLIWACK RIVER

70 MOUNT FORD

Round trip 14.5 km (9 mi)
Allow 5 hours
High point 1410 m (4620 ft)
Elevation gain 1005 m (3300 ft)
Best June to October
Map Chilliwack 92H/4

Unlike the preceding hikes in the same area, you reach the start of this one by remaining on the Chilliwack Lake Road for 2.2 km (1.4 mi) after it has recrossed to the north back of the river. Park at the end of a jeep road on the left, some 28.6 km (18 mi) east of the bridge at Vedder Crossing.

Once on foot, follow the old road upward, the fungi on it and at its sides providing interest by their sheer variety, ranging as they do in size from tiny buttons to dinner plates and in colour from purest white to deadliest black. After quite a steep ascent on the deteriorating road to about 1010 m (3300 ft), you arrive at the trail proper, marked with orange squares. This begins at road end and takes you east, after leading you left initially to north of east. Once on the ridge crest, the grade eases as you head for the summit, with only the concrete foundations remaining of the old Forest Service lookout.

As the top has been cleared of trees, you have views in all directions: north to the Lucky Four range and south to the peaks along the border, with Mount Slesse dominating its neighbours by its sheer starkness. To the east, Williams Peak stands out. The valley views have their own charms also, especially as you have the sense not only of the main river but of Foley Creek to the north, since you are on the divide between the Chilliwack River and its tributary.

Actually you may prolong your enjoyment of these sights. If you are part

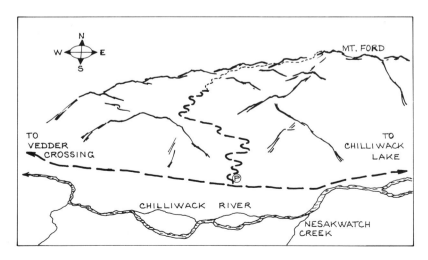

View down the cloud-filled Chilliwack Valley

of a group and can organize a two-car party, you may turn this trip into a crossover by leaving a vehicle about 4 km (2.5 mi) farther along the road at the start of the Williams Ridge Trail (Hike 71), then carrying on east along the ridge to descend there, after sampling some of the best that the Chilliwack–Foley divide has to offer. The extra traverse takes only an additional 2 hours or so; be careful, however, to note where the Williams trail leaves the ridge, as the junction may be a little obscure.

CHILLIWACK RIVER

71 WILLIAMS RIDGE

Round trip 11 km (7 mi)
Allow 6 hours
High point 1860 m (6100 ft)
Elevation gain 1415 m (4650 ft)
Best July to October
Map Chilliwack 92H/4

For the fit, or for those who want to get fit, this steep but well-marked trail is a good pipe-opener as it rises from the floor of Chilliwack River valley to the ridge over 920 m (3000 ft) above. The starting point is on the north (left) side of Chilliwack Lake Road, a little more than 32 km (20 mi) east of the Vedder Crossing bridge, or 6 km (3.7 mi) beyond the bridge on which the road recrosses to the river's north side. A sign on your left as you travel east announces it. Park here off the travelled part of the road, using the cleared area at its side.

A number of old trails and logging roads start from the same point, so care is necessary at first in following the orange markers, especially at a point about 90 metres into the bush where these fork left from a logging road and into the trees. Markers are numerous as the trail zigzags upward, mainly in forest but with some open spots to allow for breathing spaces and for enjoyment of the view across the valley as it opens up to show the grim north face of Mount Slesse, scene of an air disaster of some years ago.

On reaching the ridge proper, you see the bare rock of Williams Peak to the east. This summit serves as an indicator for a most enjoyable ridge walk of some 3.3 km (2 mi), among trees at first, then over grass and rock to the saddle that gives climbers access to the peak. A rocky knoll is the end of the

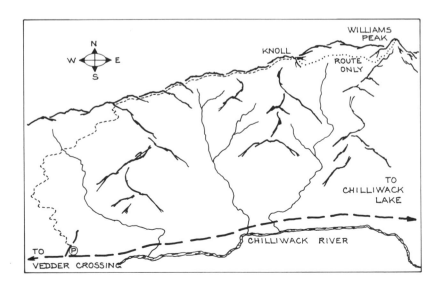

Williams Peak from Mount Ford

hiking trail; only as a member of a properly equipped party should you go farther on what is a moderately difficult climb. From your vantage point you have views of the Lucky Four peaks across Foley Creek to the northwest; Chilliwack Lake with its mountain backdrop lies to the east, and Slesse dominates the southern horizon. All in all, a satisfactory spot.

Two notes to end with: water is scarce once the snow has gone, so carry some with you. Also, check carefully the point at which the trail leaves the ridge, as it is easy to miss on your return.

CHILLIWACK RIVER

72 RADIUM LAKE

Round trip (to lake only)
  12 km (7.5 mi)
Allow 6 hours
High point 1465 m (4800 ft)
Elevation gain 885 m (2900 ft)
Best July to October
Map Skagit 92H/3

A hike on this trail takes you into high wilderness country just north of the Canada– U.S. border and south of the Chilliwack River not far from where it flows from its lake. Your turnoff comes a little short of 37 km (23 mi) from the light at Vedder Crossing bridge, or 8 km (5 mi) beyond the last crossing where the road at present loses its blacktop. Go right, then, on Paulsen Road, but take a left fork almost at once and drive to road end, just short of a ramshackle bridge over Post Creek. Cross this, and shortly afterward the main river to where the trail begins on the far bank, sharing its track with the Centennial Trail for a short distance.

First you ascend in a series of switchbacks to where the Centennial Trail goes off to the west, while you turn sharp left and continue south, following the line of an old logging road back towards the creek. Next, some steps take you up to the old road again, just above where it has been cut by a slide, and now you swing west a little then back to ascend high above the creek's west side, levelling off for a crossing after 30 minutes, one that may be awkward during periods of high water. And you are not finished with crossings, either, for after climbing east away from the creek, you turn back to return to the west side close by the foundations of an old cabin.

Thereafter, following a short spell on that bank, you return to the east

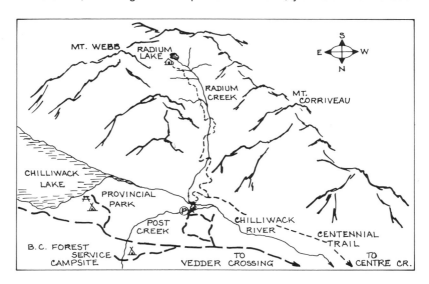

Meadows by Radium Lake – *S. Werner*

side, looking across the creek to a slide area as you rise, with a second one greeting you shortly after you have passed an old helipad. So you continue, always upward until, with one last steep pitch overcome, you reach your objective, the lake near an old cabin.

The lake's immediate surroundings are parklike, and you may follow a faint trail from the cabin to the meadows about 45 minutes beyond it; indeed, with a little extra effort you may ascend the headwall southeast to the saddle, or even to Mount Webb along the ridge to the north of that for especially fine views over Chilliwack Lake. Of course, if you have backpacked in, you may set your sights on Macdonald Peak as well, an eyrie at 2225 m (7300 ft) with unlimited views, approached easily from the same saddle. All in all, Radium Lake is a rewarding destination.

CHILLIWACK RIVER

73 GREENDROP LAKE

Round trip 14 km (9 mi)
Allow 6 hours
High point 1220 m (4000 ft)
Elevation gain 610 m (2000 ft)
Best June to October
Map Skagit 92H/3

This hike takes you over the section of the B.C. Centennial Trail covering the Chilliwack Valley end of its crossover to the Skagit, and, though it remains close to the valley bottom throughout, it provides some striking views of one-time glaciated valleys. As well, you have the two lakes, Lindeman and Greendrop, as subjects for the photographer, while its relatively low level means that it remains open when higher trails are under snow.

For a start, drive 37.7 km (23.5 mi) along the Chilliwack Lake Road and, just 1 km (0.6 mi) past Paulsen Road, turn left to the Forest Service Recreation Site at Post Creek, where you park. From here, cross the old bridge and head off north, following the creek, first on the east then the west side, reaching the near end of Lindeman Lake after some 40 minutes. Thereafter, you make your way along the lakeside via a rock slide, a forested stretch, then more rocks before the trail works it way around a steep bluff at the north end and drops to cross the creek.

On this stretch between one lake and the other, you proceed across talus slopes and through forest alternately with, eventually, the outlet from Flora Lake to negotiate, a trickle in dry spells but capable of being awkward

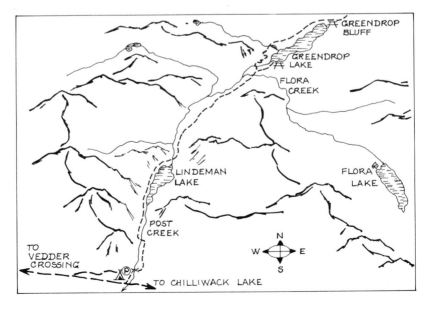

Gargoyles above Lindeman Lake

following runoff in early summer. Next you reach a fork with one trail heading for the near end of Greendrop Lake while the Centennial Trail goes left and on. Of the two, the next part of the Centennial Trail is the more interesting, since the steep sides of the lake force it to rise sharply some 215 m (700 ft) before crossing a creek which plunges precipitately to the lake. Here you may enjoy fine views of the lake and of the hanging valley opposite in which lies Flora Lake. This makes a satisfying destination for a day hike, or you may continue to the wilderness recreation site at Greendrop Bluff above the far end of the lake for views back down the Post Creek valley.

Note: During fall 1989 the old bridge over Post Creek at the Forest Service Recreation Site was washed out. In the absence of any permanent or passable bridge, you should continue on the main road a short distance beyond the creek crossing, then double back on an access road to the beginning of the trail on the east bank.

CHILLIWACK RIVER

74 FLORA LAKE

Round trip (to the lake)
  14 km (9 mi)
Allow 9 hours
High point 1770 m (5800 ft)
Elevation gain 1210 m (3975 ft)

Round trip (to pass) 12 km (7.5 mi)
Allow 6.5 hours
Elevation gain 815 m (2675 ft)
Best July to October
Map Skagit 92H/3

Like a coy lady, Flora discourages a direct approach from the Post Creek trail, preferring instead to be wooed by those prepared to hike over a 1770-m (5800-ft) pass with a drop of 395 m (1300 ft) on the other side to reach her shores. At that, the final descent and return may make this more than a comfortable day's outing, so you may be content with the ridge, which makes a very satisfactory destination.

To reach the trailhead, you drive the Chilliwack Lake Road, pass the Post Creek Recreation Site turnoff on your left, pass the Provincial Park entrance on your right and descend into the hollow about 500 metres beyond. Park in the open space on the left and hike directly into the trees to pick up the taped trail, a fine one made by a miner. On the trail, you soon come to a T-junction where you go right (left comes from another beginning a little less direct than yours).

Although your route zigzags upward in trees, you begin to have views south along the lake after little more than 30 minutes wherever the trees thin

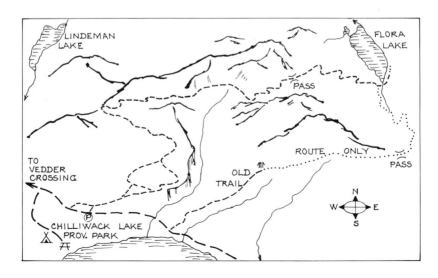

Chilliwack Lake from the trail

above the great gully to the east. As you rise, your route swings back and forth on an easy grade, using the wide slope to full advantage. En route, on the first long traverse to the west, another trail comes in from the left, an alternative whose point of divergence you may have missed on the ascent. Finally you emerge from the trees, and in the open you have no lack of views of the valley and its surrounding peaks. Then you cross an avalanche slope directly above the Provincial Park entrance, and hereafter the switchbacks become tighter as the trail steepens, until finally you round the end of the western ridge. Now the grade eases temporarily as the trail contours around the west side, then the north to reach the east side of a broad basin, crossing the first water of the day. Next it turns uphill again towards the pass, making its way backward and forward through pretty little basins and meadows interspersed with trees. Once over the pass, the trail soon drops from open heather slopes into trees, vegetation that will be with you for much of your descent to the lake. The best of your views are now behind you, to be experienced again only when you regain the pass on your return trip.

But then, what a treat is in store—a kaleidoscope of mountain scenes that vary with each change of direction, taking in on this hand or that the great peaks stretching from beyond the border south of the lake all the way down to the mouth of the Chilliwack valley. It's hard to leave such riches, but return you must eventually, perhaps trying out one or other of the miner's alternative routes; they all lead to the same end, back to the road.

Devil's Club in fruit

75 EATON LAKE

Round trip 13 km (8 mi)
Allow 6 hours
High point 1310 m (4300 ft)
Elevation gain 915 m (3000 ft)
Best June to October
Maps Hope 92H/6,
   Skagit River 92H/3

Locally this body of water is known as Crescent Lake; map-makers, however, have given it the same title as the mountain in whose shadow it lies. In fact, while it may be the destination for a day trip, it can also serve as the location for an overnight camp en route to the peaks above—those lordly eminences that look west over the Silverhope–Skagit valley, the link between the Fraser and Ross Lake in northern Washington.

Travelling east on Highway 1, turn off on the second Hope exit, then, just before the bridge over Silverhope Creek and the Riviera Motel sign, go south on Silver Skagit Road. Now you follow this road for 16.5 km (10.3 mi) as it heads upstream and crosses to the east bank of the creek. It crosses back to the west a little before a fork that precedes entrance to Silver Lake Provincial Park. Stay left here and pass to the east of the lake, then continue past the 16-km sign from the Hope business route. Just beyond the sign, turn left on an old road signposted for the Eaton Creek Forest Recreation Site. The old road soon deteriorates and narrows as new growth crowds in on this, the start of your hike.

The trail zigzags upward through tall timber, heading more or less east. On the way, it crosses Eaton Creek three times, finishing on its south side and rising from the forest into open country, with a number of large boulders strewn about like giant cannonballs. Thereafter, you soon come to

Eaton Lake from the outlet – *D. Ellis*

the lake outlet and can enjoy the sight of its waters and their mountain backdrop. Note that, if you are using this spot as a point of departure for exploring the high country, these peaks are steep: in fact, the officially named Eaton Peak (2105 m or 6900 ft) to the south involves some technical climbing.

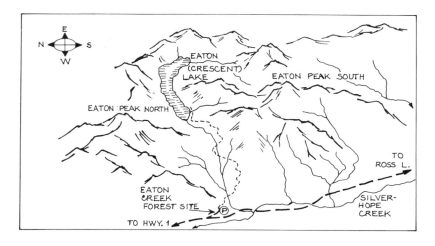

View upstream not far north of 26-Mile Bridge

SILVER-SKAGIT

76 SKAGIT RIVER TRAIL

One-way trip 14.5 km (9 mi)
Allow 6 hours
High point 625 m (2050 ft)
Elevation gain (or loss) 105 m (350 ft)
Best June to October
Map Skagit River 92H/3

If you are fortunate, you will hit the brief mid-June flowering of rhododendrons on this trail, but even without that bonus, the trip from the Silver Skagit Road at 26-Mile Bridge, following the route of the historic Whatcom Trail upstream to Highway 3 at the western end of Manning Park, is a rewarding one as is the corresponding downstream hike. For complete success, however, it does require the organization of a two-car party with a key exchange at mid-point, otherwise you must cut your trip short unless you are prepared for a 29-km (18-mi) march there and back.

For the downstream end of this interesting trail, drive 42.8 km (26.7 mi) along the Silver Skagit Road from just west of Hope, crossing the Skagit River and parking at the picnic site on its far side. Thereafter, you walk south along the road for a short distance before going left on a wide, signposted track with trees on either side, one that leads after about 20 minutes to a T-junction. Here you go left (the Centennial Trail continues right) past a Forest Service growth plot on the left and through several clusters of rhododendrons before surmounting a bluff with splendid views of Silvertip Mountain and its little glacier.

Next you must negotiate a low-lying stretch which the river floods at high water, then, having crossed Twenty-eight Mile Creek, you enter an Ecological Reserve set aside for its magnificent cedars and Douglas-firs. Your trip through the reserve, as you wind your way amongst these forest giants, both standing and fallen, lasts for about 40 minutes, so you have ample time to admire and enjoy. Proceeding onward, you may notice on your right hand some large boulders, erratics dumped by a glacier in retreat. Then comes your crossing of Twenty-six Mile Creek with, a few minutes north of the bridge, a faint trail leading to another rhododendron cluster; you may want to turn aside and visit it.

Should you be continuing your upstream trip, you will go right following your little excursion, and in a little over an hour cross Silverdaisy Creek, beyond which there is another possible brief sidetrip to a waterfall and mine. Next, the trail to Silverdaisy Mountain (Hike 91) goes off on your right, and shortly after, you come to the crossing of the Skagit River itself, with the parking area at Sumallo Grove close by.

To reach this spot from Highway 1, stay with the freeway past Hope and go off on Highway 3 at its parting from Highway 5. From there, turn off after 25.8 km (16 mi) to Sumallo Grove near the confluence of the Sumallo and the Skagit rivers.

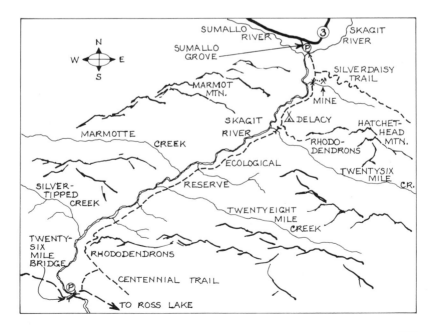

165

From the Skyline southwest across the border – *D. Ellis*

SILVER-SKAGIT

77 SKYLINE TRAIL WEST

Round trip (to Camp Mowich)
26 km (16 mi)
Allow 10 hours or overnight
High point 1830 m (6000 ft)
Elevation gain 1310 m (4300 ft)
Best July to October
Maps Manning Park 92H/2,
Skagit River 92 H/3

In its entirety, Skyline Trail links the Skagit Valley Recreation Area with Manning Park, descending from the high country to the Gibson Pass Road at either Strawberry Flats or Lightning Lakes (Hike 96). At its western end, however, its beginning elevation is much lower, so the complete trip from west to east is a long day indeed, even for parties who have arranged transportation at each end with an exchange of keys en route. Still, the casual hiker or backpacker need not be discouraged from going part way and returning, with Camp Mowich (meaning "deer") near the midpoint giving access to alpine ridge walking for overnighters.

To reach the departure point, you must travel south on the Silver Skagit Road for 54.6 km (34 mi) from its beginning west of Hope to park in the new trailhead area on the left. Once on foot, you head east in open forest across the level floor of the valley, in a zone transitional between the coastal vegetation and that of the drier Interior. After several minutes' pleasant walking, you are joined by the Centennial Trail from the west and subsequently the two trails are one as you begin to rise, crossing the first of the creeks that you must negotiate. Once on its south side, you follow it for a short time before your route veers off right and you traverse the first of two raised benches indicative of one-time lake levels. Next you find yourself heading into the valley of a second creek, with a series of Parks Branch switchbacks to greet you once you re-emerge, turning from south to east in the process. All this time you have been rising steadily through tall forest with only two spots to provide viewpoints to the outside world. Now, however, the trees thin out as you approach the subalpine meadows, glorious in late July and August. Finally, on the last ridge before you descend to the headwaters of Mowich Creek, you are in the true alpine, with vistas galore on which to feast your eyes; across Ross Lake to the peaks around Mount Redoubt, along the ridge to the stately spires of Hozomeen Mountain nearby, and past the summits of Frosty Mountain to the gentle rolling landscape in the north. At over 1615 m (5300 ft) and 8.5 km (5.3 mi) from the start, this would make a suitable destination for the day hiker.

From here to the camp you cross the long north ridge of Hozomeen (though in Canada it is Hozameen) Mountain, the eastern section of the trail stretching out ahead along the south slopes of Lone Goat Mountain and beyond. You, however, must swing around the head of one creek before losing 150 m (500 ft) to reach Mowich, its main advantage being the presence of water that is otherwise in short supply on the alpine ridges. With a day or so at your disposal, you may make a trip south along Hozomeen's ridge or, using the northward extension of the same ridge, head for Nepopekum's gentle summit.

Your return, once you have regained your height across the ridge from the camp, is downhill all the way, and it will surely take a lot less than the six hours or so that you required for your ascent.

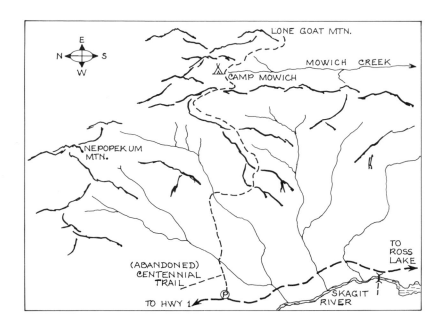

78 GALENE LAKES

Round trip 32 km (20 mi)
Allow 11 hours or overnight
High point 1755 m (5750 ft)
Elevation gain 1250 m (4700 ft)
Best late July to October
Map Skagit River 92H/3

After having been cut off for a number of years by the destruction of the original logging bridge, this fine alpine area is accessible once again via the new Chittenden Bridge over the Skagit River. The only drawback is that this crossing is some distance downstream from the trail, adding more than an hour to the one-way hike and making an overnight trip advisable either by backpacking to the lakes or by camping in one of the valley's nearby sites (e.g., Hozomeen) to get an early start.

To reach the beginning of your hike, leave Highway 1 just west of Hope on the Silverhope exit and drive south on Silver Skagit Road for nearly 58 km (36 mi) to the Chittenden Bridge, then another 200 metres to a parking area on the left. After crossing the grand new bridge, go straight ahead on the track to the Chittenden meadows. There you turn smartly right and follow the road north, deviating neither to left nor to right until near its end you turn right down to the river with its gravel bar, a nice stop for a short rest with a fine view of Hozomeen Mountain.

The trail, continuing north, now takes you through its least pleasant part, a stretch close enough to the river to be muddy at high water, then over an

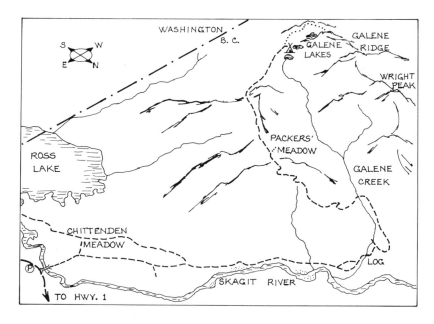

New Chittenden Bridge

old rockfall before emerging on a washed-out road on which you proceed, finally turning uphill to meet the road again after a cut-off. Then you cross the forks of Galene Creek, the north one on an immense tree trunk and, heading up to the top of its north bank, follow the track along it until you emerge on the old road once more.

This you follow to its end and the start of an old mining pack trail, still in remarkably good condition, apart from some deadfalls higher up. So you proceed in deep forest, the ground moss-covered; there are even—surprise —clusters of rhododendrons to greet you. On your way back into the valley, you cross two small tributaries, the damp space around them encouraging devil's club for you to avoid. This stretch ends with recrossing the creek, using whatever means possible.

From now on there are more deadfalls, but stay with the trail as it rounds the ridge then climbs steadily to the open alpine meadows, traversing a sidehill with spectacular views to the mountains east of Ross Lake and south into the Cascade wilderness. Next you follow a narrow ridge, at the end of which you turn sharp right, arriving at the middle lake where camping is possible in the vicinity of the remains of some old cabins.

Staying overnight gives you a chance to explore this area, enjoying the alpine flowers appropriate to the time of your visit: yellow avalanche lilies arriving with the departing snow in July, followed by a riotous kaleidoscope of colour in the high season. A trip to the ridge above your camp via the grassy spur to your left gives you this added bounty of unspoiled meadow with the sight of the remote upper lake as yet another prize for your efforts.

FRASER CANYON

79 MOUNT LINCOLN

Round trip 5 km (3.25 mi)
Allow 3.5 hours
High point 655 m (2150 ft)
Elevation gain 580 m (1900 ft)
Best April to October
Map Spuzzum 92H/11

Just east and north of the village of Yale is a dome pierced by Highway 1: this is Mount Lincoln. Although quite steep, it does have a rough track up it; one or two exposed places are fitted with standing ropes to give you confidence. From the summit you have fine views over the little townsite and along the canyon with its road and two railway tracks, one on either side.

Going north, drive through the village and park at the Historic Yale sign at a turnout where the old road—branching right from the new one—crosses the CPR tracks. Walk north for about 100 metres towards a large boulder just beyond the point where the highway crosses a small creek. A little to the left of this rock, a faint trail leads off uphill, soon becoming a graded zig-zag track that ascends steadily, sometimes on scree, sometimes on grass.

After about 40 minutes you come to the first rope on a sharp incline, and 20 minutes more brings you to the second. Shortly after, a third rope enables you to negotiate an exposed bare rockface, but after that the slope eases off and you have time to look around you. Now comes your final scramble to the summit with its TV relay station for the town below, which would otherwise be bereft of this form of entertainment because of the mountains. Your route, in fact, is probably used for servicing the station, as you are fairly close to the cable all the way.

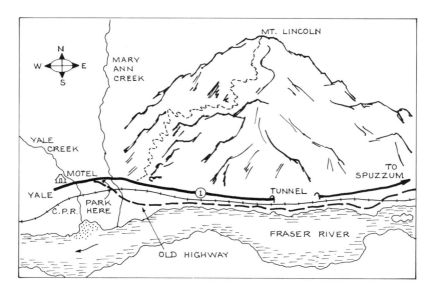

Routes to the coast, by river, rail and road

On the top, besides admiring the view, you may indulge in a little retrospective fantasy, calling up scenes from the time when this was a busy river port, the head of Fraser navigation and the transfer point for supplies to the Cariboo goldfields during the stirring days of 1859.

However, this trail is for experienced hikers, and if you do find it too challenging, you have as an alternative Spirit Caves Trail to the south of the village. For it, drive back 2 km (1.2 mi) to the Pioneer Cemetery marker opposite which the trail begins, a small plaque announcing its creation in 1973.

FRASER CANYON

80 FIRST BRIGADE TRAIL

Round trip 13 km (8 mi)
Allow 5 hours
High point 900 m (2950 ft)
Elevation gain 730 m (2400 ft)
Best June to October
Maps Spuzzum 92H/11, Boston Bar 92H/14

For anyone exploring the Fraser Canyon region, this walk is a must; not only is it attractive scenically, it also allows the hiker to retrace one of the earliest pioneer routes to the Interior. This link with B.C.'s colourful past dates to 1848, in fact, when A. C. Anderson of the Hudson's Bay Company set out to establish a route to the north and east overland from Yale.

Today, cars roar up and down the Trans-Canada Highway, those heading inland crossing the Fraser from west bank to east on the fine high-level Alexandra Bridge. Just north of the bridge on the east side of the highway is Alexandra Lodge, the one-time 14-Mile House, now a heritage building, beside which the original trail started. Today, however, it begins some 300 metres north, midway up a long hill. Parking is available on the same side of the highway about 150 metres beyond the trailhead, or opposite it in a cleared area on the west (river) side. Before you set off, or perhaps on your return, stroll over to the edge; the view up the Fraser is particularly fine here. The trail itself begins by a small stream and climbs in a series of zigzags in open timber, rising above the road and heading mainly east. As it climbs, the forest cover thins for a time. Eventually the trail crosses an old rock slide before reaching a high, open bluff with views of the river in its valley and of the peaks along the canyon's west side. This is a good spot to rest and enjoy the scene.

From here on, your ascent is much gentler as the trail continues in open timber along a ridge leading somewhat east of north. Eventually you reach a small lake, near which is the conjectured site of Lake House, the first stopping point en route for the Anderson River valley. Carry on north from here, till your route, turning west a little, comes out on a high bluff overlooking the canyon. This is a suitable destination if you are returning by the same way.

If you have a two-car party, a recommended alternative is to make this trip a crossover. Continue north along the bluffs, finally linking up with the 1858 Trail (see Hike 81) and descending to the highway some 5 km (3 mi) north of your original point of setting out. Your time from the observation point should be about 75 minutes, though you may take longer because of the succession of fine views of that important traffic artery between B.C.'s coast and its Interior, the Fraser Canyon.

Along the Bluffs Trail

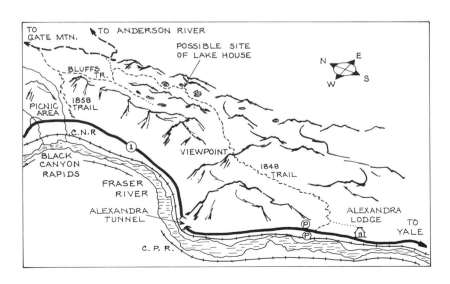

FRASER CANYON

81 GATE MOUNTAIN

Round trip 16 km (10 mi)
Allow 7 hours
High point 1450 m (4760 ft)
Elevation gain 1175 m (3850 ft)
Best June to October
Maps Spuzzum 92H/11,
Boston Bar 92H/14

Like the preceding hike immediately to the south, this one uses an old pack trail, one established in 1858, at the time of the gold rush to the Fraser River and the Cariboo. In view of its steepness, one can only feel sorry for the mules that had to carry loads over the ridge between the Fraser and the Anderson River to the east, while admiring the determination of the men who refused to be stopped by the natural difficulties associated with the bluffs above Hell's Gate.

Travelling north on today's highway, you ascend a long hill beginning just after Alexandra Tunnel. Near the top of this, as the road narrows, a small creek descends from the right, and where it passes under the highway is Cooper's Corner Rest Area, a possible parking spot 5.3 km (3.3 mi) north of Alexandra Lodge. From here, however, you must walk back along the shoulder of the busy road until, just past the sixth power pole from your start, you pick up the markers. Note that this point is almost opposite the north end of a wide pullout, another possible parking spot, one that obviates the need to walk the narrow shoulder.

The route itself, adorned with tape and orange markers, ascends steeply for the first 600 m (2000 ft) or so in a series of switchbacks, making an early start advisable to avoid the heat of the day. As you climb, the grade eases a little before you intersect with Bluffs Trail—the connecting link with the 1848

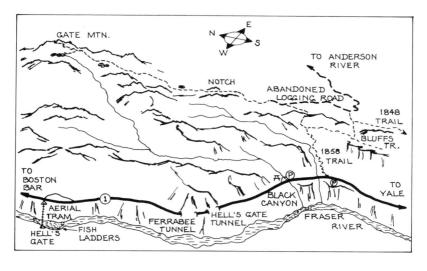

East beyond the Anderson River

Trail—that joins from the right. After going left and rising a little more, the markers lead you slightly to the right into a bushy draw before veering left (north) again on a very faint trail through open forest. Next, you meet the old access road for the abandoned lookout and here, at present, the orange markers end.

Stay with the road to its end, enjoying wild strawberries in season, then turn left and steeply up the ridge, the trail now marked here and there with tapes. Following the trail up the ridge to a minor summit, "The Notch," at almost 1220 m (4000 ft), you have a possible destination if you think that another 90 minutes is beyond you, especially as the trail from here on is somewhat bushy with a few windfalls. If you do advance from here, you pass one or two minor summits on your left as you remain generally on the east side of the ridge, then, after one last draw, you find yourself on the rocky summit with its deserted lookout.

The view that greets you is panoramic: the Fraser Canyon stretches north and south, the Anderson River system lies spread out to the east and southeast; in the distance to the south stand Hope Mountain and the Holy Cross Peak, and Mount Urquhart rises proudly in the southwest. And when you stop feasting your eyes on distant scenes and look downward, there, just below you, is a small lake, which you may wish to visit on your return journey by way of a short detour west.

FRASER CANYON

82 STEIN RIVER TRAIL

High point (Stein Lake)
  1035 m (3400 ft)
Elevation gain 765 m (2500 ft)
High point (cable crossing)
  590 m (1930 ft)
Elevation gain 315 m (1030 ft)
Best May to October
Map Stein River 92I/5

Two approaches to the Stein River watershed, by Blowdown and Lizzie Creeks, have already been described in this book. Here is the obvious route, going upstream from its confluence with the Fraser a short distance north of Lytton but on the opposite side of the river from that community. It involves an interesting ferry crossing: the craft uses a cable to harness the swift current.

To reach the ferry, follow Highway 12 through Lytton, cross the Thompson River on its single-lane bridge, then go left at the ferry sign some 800 metres beyond. The ferry itself runs on call from early morning to after 10 p.m., with two half-hour breaks, one in the forenoon, the other in early evening, and though the trip takes only five minutes, you may have to wait, since the little craft carries only two vehicles at a time. Once on the west bank, turn right and, ignoring one road going off left, travel 1.6 km (1 mi) to the entrance of Earlscourt Farm and turn off West Side Road here. In recent years, an arrangement with the owners has been made, thus avoiding the earlier approach via the Indian Reservation farther north. Hikers can help repay this kindness by staying on the posted trail, closing gates after them, and leaving no garbage.

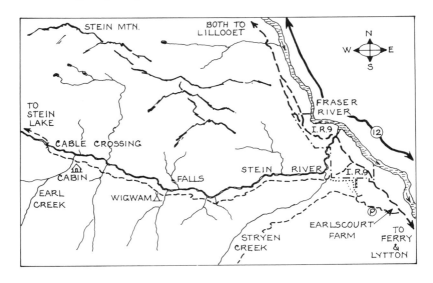

Cable ferry crossing at Lytton

Turn left on the farm road, therefore, following the orange squares (some have faded already), sign the trail register and proceed to the parking spot by an old orchard. From here you follow a gated track north, your way made cheerful with flowers. En route you rise from one bench to another, a powerline over to your left. Next, in a cluster of trees, you come to a posted junction where Stryen Creek Trail stays left while you continue forward on a track over a field, gradually converging with the powerline. Finally you swing west, the meadow ends, and you traverse a stretch of burned-over ponderosa, its redeeming features being the young growth springing up to hide the scars and the view you get up the valley. Here you join the original trail as you drop to cross Stryen Creek not far from its confluence with the Stein.

From now on, keeping the Stein on your right, you stay on the river flats except where you have to rise over canyon walls and steep cliffs. For a day trip you may make your destination "The Wigwam," with its teepee poles, situated on a large river flat, a 7 hour round trip of over 16 km (10 mi) from the start.

Should you continue upstream, you will find yourself rising to bench level, then descending towards the river again, after which you reach Earl cabin and a tributary of the Stein bearing the same name. A long day's hike of some 27 km (16.8 mi), about 10 hours for the round trip, takes you to the cable crossing of the main river, a possible overnight stopping place also if you are backpacking. In fact, with time and energy at your disposal, you may make this the first stop of a seven- or eight-day return trip to Stein Lake now that the trail has been upgraded and the river crossings improved. Before embarking on the latter, however, it would be wise to check with the Outdoor Recreation Council (687-3333) for the latest developments.

Don't forget that the Stein is sacred to the Lytton Indians and features largely in their traditions. Treat it and its surroundings, therefore, with respect. For more information on this fascinating area consult **Exploring the Stein River Valley** by Roger Freeman and David Thompson (1979).

83 BOTANIE MOUNTAIN

Round trip 17.5 km (11 mi)
Allow 8 hours
High point 2000 m (6550 ft)
Elevation gain 1425 m (4650 ft)
Best June to October
Map Lytton 92I/4

Travellers heading north and east past Lytton on Highway 1 cannot fail to be aware of the great spine on their left, the ridge that serves to divide the waters of the Fraser from those of the Thompson. The exotic-sounding name, too, is romantic, conjuring up visions of intriguing plants. It is therefore something of an anticlimax to find that the original spelling was "Boothanie," a reference in the Indian tongue to the mist that so often enshrouds the area. Still, the mountain slopes are famous for wild flowers, so perhaps there is justification for the spelling.

To reach the ridge with its B.C. Forest Service lookout, leave Highway 1 and follow the signs for Highway 12 into Lytton. Take the road to Lillooet till after it crosses the Thompson River just above its confluence with the Fraser. Some 400 metres north of the bridge, fork right on the signposted Botanie Valley Road and stay with it as it parallels the north bank of the Thompson for some distance before it starts rising and swinging away from the river. Then, just as you start to turn into the valley at about 3 km (1.8 mi) from your fork, a striking vertical rockface to the right claims your attention. It is worth stopping on the wide pullout at the highest corner to gaze across at the great cliff and to look down on the hoodoos (rock pillars left by erosion) on the canyon's near side. Continuing into the wide upper valley with its extensive irrigation, at 6.8 km (4.2 mi) from your original turnoff you come on a deteriorating dirt road going uphill to the left. This you may drive for about 600 metres, but there are parking spots earlier if you wish to stop

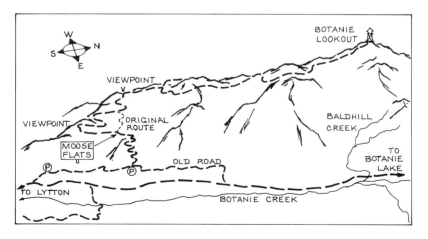

North up the Fraser River to Botanie Mountain

before the junction where your route, a track even more deteriorated, goes off uphill left.

This jeep track climbs steeply up the side of the ridge with many zigzags, some of the steep corners providing interesting views of Botanie valley and the north end of the Fraser Canyon. After about 45 minutes, and just past a sign reading Moose Flats, watch for the original road on the right. Although shorter and steeper than the present road, it has more shade and is pleas-anter underfoot, especially in hot weather. Finally, at an altitude of about 1200 m (4000 ft), you reach the ridge. With this you stay, more or less, as the track takes you to a lookout about 5 km (3 mi) along the crest, at first among trees, but later on open rock. Here is a satisfying destination with im-pressive mountain views to the west on both sides of the Stein Valley. East and south, too, the eye follows the line of the two great main rivers to their junction at Lytton, the clear water of the Thompson contrasting vividly with the silt-laden Fraser.

Although the lookout is not the true summit of the mountain, the latter is not recommended, as approach to it involves a descent of 215 m (700 ft) into a col and an extra 5 km (3 mi) of walking, while the Forest Service tower gives just as good views with far less effort. In any event, it is a sufficiently long hike to this point; dry, too, in summer.

COQUIHALLA

84 THE NEEDLE

Round trip 13 km (8 mi)
Allow 6 hours
High point 2105 m (6900 ft)
Elevation gain 855 m (2900 ft)
Best July to September
Map Spuzzum 92H/11

Recognizing its potential for recreation, the Provincial Parks and Outdoor Recreation Division is formulating plans for the provision of combined viewpoints and trailheads around the high point of Highway 5 (Coquihalla Highway), one south of Boston Bar Summit, one at 1230 m (4000 ft) on the divide itself, and the third about 4 km (2.5 mi) beyond it at Fallslake Creek. At each of these, an underpass gives access to the opposite side of the divided highway, the first and third permitting vehicles, the other for pedestrians only.

It must be stressed that no development of hiking trails has so far taken place; a few routes, however, are already possible for experienced groups. Still, it must be remembered that this is high country with heavy snowfall, and mist can reduce visibility almost to zero in a few minutes, a definite hazard on unmarked routes. With these provisos, however, here is a hike from Zopkios Ridge Lookout (or rather, from the highway works yard on the opposite side of the road to it) taking you to the east and into the area between the valley of Boston Bar Creek and the Coquihalla. This ridge culminates in The Needle, a name indicative of its sharp appearance; however, the ridge is reward in itself, so no feats of mountaineering are called for.

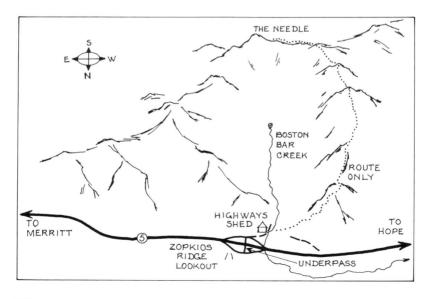

Along the ridge to the Needle

So what's the snag? Well, at present no trail exists to get you through the forest to the end of the ridge, so having crossed the creek at the west end of the works yard, you must make your way up contending with a tangle of bush for the first 300 m (1000 ft) or so—a procedure that may be good for the soul but is hard on the temper. To avoid the worst of the bush, head directly for the ridge to the west and work south up the crest. Towards the end of this stage signs of better things to come manifest themselves as patches of grass and heather become interspersed with the trees. Now, too, the grade eases, and you are soon striding along in fine subalpine surroundings, which in turn give way to the purely alpine. From here on, the hike is sheer pleasure as you make your way over granite slabs and heathery meadows, with views of The Needle and its precipitous ridges ahead and the peaks with the Himalayan animal names to your rear, a foretaste of the view on the return trip.

Finally, at about 1850 m (6000 ft), the ridge you have been following southward merges with that from the west and you change direction towards the peak, which is easier to climb than its name suggests, though it does involve some scrambling. Finding the right gully, of two leading to the summit, is also a problem, both ascending and descending, so perhaps you may want to rest on your laurels once you reach the base. If, however, you decide to press on, do take time to search out the easier route on the right and to note its position for your return.

COQUIHALLA

85 ZOA PEAK

Round trip 11 km (7 mi)
Allow 6 hours
High point 1875 m (6150 ft)
Elevation gain 625 m (2050 ft)
Best July to October
Map Spuzzum 92H/11

Of the hikes in the high divide area of Highway 5, this one is, for now at least, the most appealing. Not only is the bush light but the grade is generally gentle, though you do have to lose some height to get from one prong to the other of the double summit. The picturesque name of the peak owes its origins to a B.C. mountaineer who in naming the mountains of this area chose the names of animals indigenous to the alpine regions of central Asia, Zoa being one of the yak family.

Falls Lake Trailhead, 1.3 km (0.8 mi) north of Highway 5, is your starting point for this outing. Turn off left towards Falls Lake from the old Coldwater road a short distance northeast of the parking area by the creek and ascend a sharp little rise. At the top, where the Falls Lake road turns left, you go right along the pipeline on what looks like a very overgrown old road. The appearance is worse than the reality, however, and soon you are painlessly gaining height as you head east on a rudimentary trail along the right-of-way. On this you stay for approximately 30 minutes to where the pipeline starts to curve around the ridge and before the forest above it thickens. Here on your left you should look for a dry creek; this is your approach and as you ascend on it you realize you are on a faint, though intermittent, trail. Thus you rise, avoiding clusters of bush and coming on a few tapes that will give you a rough direction, though actually all you need do is follow the ridge upward. As you ascend, trees thin out and you travel in pleasant sub-

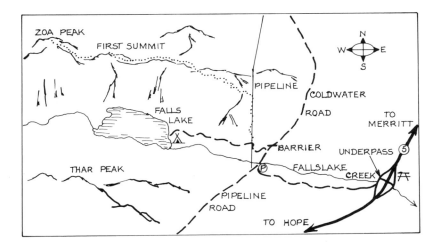

Northwest from the main summit

alpine country to the first summit at just over 1850 m (6000 ft), with a glorious view, almost panoramic, for your efforts. To complete the picture you must lose 54 m (175 ft)—and regain it—to reach the second summit, a large, relatively flat area with trees, meadows and excellent views to west and north, the starkness of the nearby "animal" peaks being particularly impressive.

Should you wish to stay overnight, the hike to this mountain and its immediate neighbour, Thar Peak, may be undertaken from Falls Lake, for which a walk-in campsite is planned. There is already (in 1986) a camping spot at the east end of the lake, but it is unorganized and poorly cared for by its users, so for the present your expectations should be aimed low to avoid disappointment.

Thar Peak from the east

COQUIHALLA

86 THAR PEAK

Round trip (from Fallslake Creek)
5 km (3 mi)
Allow 4 hours

Round trip (from Zopkios Lookout)
7 km (4.5 mi)
Allow 5 hours
High point 1920 m (6300 ft)
Elevation gain 700 m (2300 ft)
Best July to early October
Map Spuzzum 92H/11

If the ascent to The Needle's north ridge was bushy, this climb may suffer from overmuch exposure, for this east-facing ridge has few trees on it at all; there is also no water in summer, so an early start with some liquid in your pack is recommended. At present, of course, a defined trail is lacking, but that is a want that will eventually be filled either by Parks staff activity or by the feet of individual users.

Your objective here is the most northerly peak of Zopkios Ridge, the name (like others in the area) that of an alpine herbivorous creature, adopted as late as 1975, some indication of how remote this region was until relatively recently. For it, or for a scramble to the peak of Nak, its higher neighbour to the southwest, one possible point of access is the Falls Lake trailhead, 1.3 km (0.8 mi) north of the Falls Lake exit from Highway 5. Here, just west of the parking area by the creek, a pipeline road goes steeply uphill.

On this you soon round the end of the east ridge of Thar and approach the high point of this section of the pipeline road, after which you should watch for the easiest route up the ridge, avoiding as best you can the fringe of bush lying between the road and the open rocky slope.

Another approach via the basin between Nak and Thar is also accessible from the Boston Bar Summit, which you reach by driving about 3 km (2 mi) to the first exit south of the Falls Lake one. And here you find the pipeline road again, slanting uphill just east of the southbound parking area.

Quite soon after you start rising and not long after a spectacular glimpse of Yak Peak, you strike off upward, angling a little right to avoid some bluffs then heading into the high basin that opens up as you ascend, finally swinging right towards the peak. From Thar the view is awe-inspiring, especially on the steep north side, frowning down on Falls Lake and across at the precipitous south flank of Zoa.

Your return may be by the same route back to your starting point; however, Provincial Parks has plans for a crossover, an attractive possibility, simplifying route-finding as well.

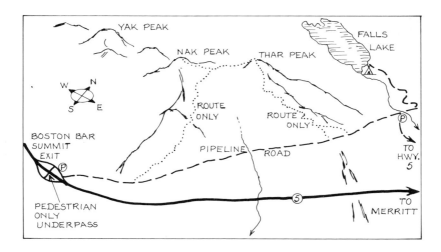

COQUIHALLA

87 MOUNT HENNING

Round trip 10.5 km (6.5 mi) or more
Allow 5 hours or more
High point 1830 m (6000 ft)
Elevation gain 730 m (2400 ft)

Round trip (loop only) 8 km (5 mi)
Allow 3.5 hours
High point 1645 m (5400 ft)
Elevation gain 550 m (1800 ft)
Best July to October
Maps Tulameen 92H/10,
      Spuzzum 92H/11

Parsimonious hikers from the Lower Mainland may feel aggrieved that the approach to this pleasant high-country area is just beyond the tollgates on the new Highway 5. Still, it serves as a prelude to the other fine hikes in the Merritt area; in fact, it may be the overture to them. Having paid over your dues, therefore, you look for the Coquihalla Lakes Exit to the right as you swoop down the hill after the tollbooth. At the cattle grid, turn right again, then go left on the new Tulameen Forest Road. Next, you go left on the second narrow dirt road beyond the fork. Stay left at the next split, left again, then go right before parking at the next fork, all within 1 km (0.6 mi) of your turnoff for Tulameen.

Set out by taking the left fork across a small creek on a cat road, probably constructed to fight a forest fire, the signs of which were clearly visible on

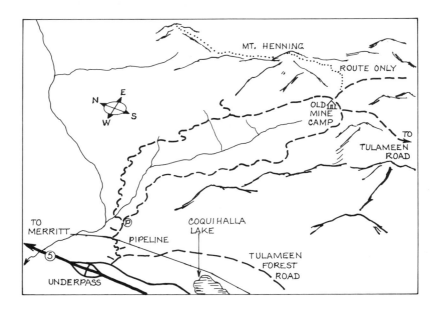

Remains of Independence Mine camp

your approach. Following the easy grade upward allows you to enjoy the wide-open vista, from Coquihalla Mountain on the left, the canyon of the same name straight ahead beyond the lakes, and Highway 5 snaking off right towards Boston Bar Creek, with the stark peaks of Zopkios Ridge providing a backdrop to the whole dramatic scene.

Once past the burnt-over area, the trail reverts to its former mine road status, turning towards a wooded ridge in the process, and giving evidence of use by cattle, bears, and trail bikers as well as hikers. Next comes a fork, with the left-hand track going up the slope, while you continue into the pass and to the one dilapidated shack, all that is left of the one-time Independence Mine Camp (another cabin has fallen victim to fire). From here you head uphill for the open ridge of which Mount Henning is the highest bump. Up on the crest the views of distant peaks and valleys all around and the meadows underfoot make it hard to resist the urge to wander on and on. There is no trail on the ridge, but its openness makes one unnecessary. The main thing to watch for is the point at which you gained it, so that you may descend by the same route to the cabin for your return.

Back there, to complete the loop, first take the track to the right (south), then almost immediately go right again, working west around the head of the valley to descend on its south side, reaching your vehicle by the other fork from that on which you set out. It has to be admitted, however, that this route is less scenic than the other, lying as it does mainly among trees, but it does give a circular trip and a shady return on a hot day.

88 MOUNT THYNNE

Round trip (from shed)
10.5 km (6.5 mi)
Allow 5 hours
High point 2028 (6649 ft)
Elevation gain 305 m (1000 ft)
Best July to early October
Maps Tulameen 92H/10,
Aspen Grove 92H/15

Purist hikers will undoubtedly wish to try the one-time pack trail to the B.C. Forest Service lookout atop this commanding mountain, a one-way journey of 17.5 km (11 mi) with a vertical rise of 1190 m (3900 ft). Lesser mortals, however, are not deprived of the pleasure to be gained by a successful ascent, the difference being in the use of a service road for two contemporary telecommunication towers to reduce significantly the length of the hike.

If you belong in the latter category, your adventure begins with your leaving Highway 5 on the Coldwater Road at the Brookmere exit 29 km (18 mi) south of Merritt. Follow the sign to Brookmere and you are soon on a good gravel road gradually turning away from the new superhighway. After 10 km (6 mi), you cross the CPR tracks in this one-time bustling railway centre, its tall water tower still bearing mute testimony to the days of steam. Just before a second crossing, you go right, and now you are on a logging road with the restrictions on weekday travel thus entailed. On it, you pass one right fork, but take the next after nearly 7 km (4.3 mi), then follow another right just over 3 km (1.9 mi) beyond.

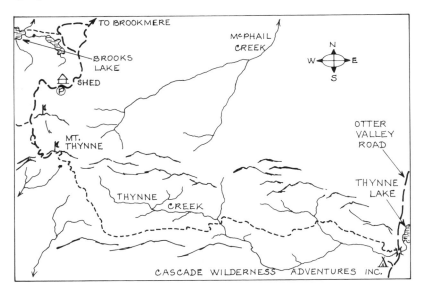

Old Forest Service lookout

By this time you are in the open, the result of logging, and your destination is visible but still some distance off, and now you do go left, leaving the logging road for the rougher microwave service road. How far you drive on this, of course, depends on your vehicle and your inclination; certainly you may drive past the two successive roads going off to the right to Brooks Lake Forest Service Recreation Area. Thereafter, however, you have the first really awkward bit of road, and, a little beyond that, a shed on a flat stretch with ample parking space precedes a very steep and rough hill. Here you may well wish to leave your car and take to foot, almost 5 km (3 mi) since you left the logging road. As you press on uphill, a microwave tower looms up on the left, but this is still some distance below your objective, which heaves into view as you come onto the ridge for the last scenic stretch of your trek.

Once on top, though, you will not want to waste time gazing at CN installations; instead, you may set off along the south ridge to an area dotted with little lakes and with fine views to south and west. And having paid your respects here, you may work back around to the southeast just below the summit, passing the old Forest Service lookout and noting the upper end of the pack trail, its top section tastefully bordered with native rock, before it disappears into the trees of the basin below, a far cry from its beginning behind the camp operated by Cascade Wilderness Adventures just south of Thynne Lake on the Otter Valley road (gravel), 14.4 km (9 mi) north of Tulameen and some 35 km (22 mi) from Brookmere.

COQUIHALLA

89 STOYOMA MOUNTAIN

Round trip 12 km (7.5 mi)
Allow 5 hours
High point 2283 m (7486 ft)
Elevation gain 670 m (2190 ft)
Best July to September
Maps Boston Bar 92H/14,
Prospect Creek 92I/3

The new Highway 5 from Hope to Merritt has put the graceful double summit of Stoyoma within reach of the weekend hiker from the Lower Mainland, perhaps using the site at Cabin Lake or the Forest Service campsite at Lightning Lake for an overnight stay. In Merritt, stay left on Highway 8, the road to Spence's Bridge, where it leaves Highway 5 at a traffic light. From this point drive 18.7 km (11.7 mi) to the Petit Creek turnoff. This is on the left of the road and is not easily seen; however, if you do come in sight of the bridge across the Nicola River, you have overshot it (it is easier to pick up coming from the west).

If half the pleasure of an outing is getting there, then this one must rank high, as you travel south on wide, well-graded logging roads. At 23.1 km (14.5 mi), having swung west away from Spius Creek, you reach Prospect Creek Bridge. Here you cross the creek and, almost immediately, stay left to cross Miner Creek. Just after the 35-km marker (put in by the logging company), you fork right off the mainline road and shortly thereafter go right again. Immediately after a shelter belt of trees 1.4 km (0.9 mi) from your first right turnoff, park where you see an old track going off right.

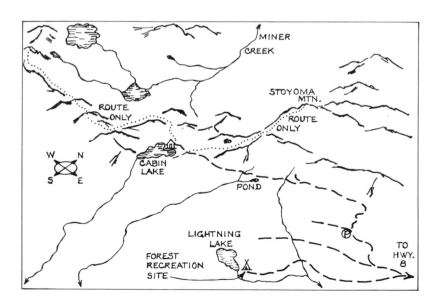

Twin summits of Stoyoma from the logging road

On this one-time cattle road, you cross a logged area, then gradually contour to the south, returning to forest as you advance. Even so, there are sufficient openings to allow distant views as you proceed, travelling more or less at right angles to the tail of the mountain's gentle south ridge. On the way you pass a fork to your right, but to get to the ridge proper, you are better to use the second of two draws if you are anxious to start right away; the best route, however, comes just before your trail drops down to a lake, unnamed on the map but popularly known as Cabin Lake, a cabin and such amenities as a biffy and a picnic table by its north shore giving ample reason for the name.

From the track's high point at 1880 m (6170 ft), ascend to the north through the bleached stems of the burned-over forest to the open ridge above, but not before you have admired an attractive-looking ridge on the other side of the valley in which the lake is situated. As you go higher, Mount Hewitt Bostock rears its impressive head over to your left, but your route towards the gentle south summit over open meadows presents no answering challenge. The north summit is more demanding, at least towards the west, but it too has a long gentle ridge approach if you wish to tackle both. And on a fine day, with vistas stretching to the horizon and pretty meadow underfoot, you will undoubtedly want to prolong your visit to this pleasant area before returning to Cabin Lake for your walk down the road to your car.

With a second day at your disposal, you may add to your itinerary a hike along the fine open ridge running west from Cabin Lake. From the crest you look down on several lakes, the headwaters of Miner Creek, lying between Stoyoma to the northeast and its companion, Mount Hewitt Bostock, to the northwest.

HOPE-MANNING PARK

90 MOUNT OUTRAM

Round trip 16 km (10 mi)
Allow 9 hours
High point 2440 m (8000 ft)
Elevation gain 1785 m (5850 ft)
Best July to September
Maps Skagit 92H/3, Hope 92H/6

For this mountain—named after a nineteenth-century British general who apparently never saw B.C. in his life—the approach is located at the western entrance to Manning Park, 18.1 km (11.3 mi) east of the junction of Highways 3 and 5. Here a parking lot, its entrance adorned with a large carved beaver effigy, is the trailhead. From it two switchbacks take you up to a long-abandoned road on which you turn right to cross a talus slope. Then you descend slightly before going left on the trail signposted for Mount Outram, your route lying in deep forest.

In the main, the going is quite steep as you rise in a series of short switchbacks, so that the crossing of Seventeen Mile Creek at 1675 m (5500 ft) gives a good excuse for a rest, especially as the tree cover has thinned on your approach to the subalpine zone, and you can now enjoy some views. The route, well marked with tapes and cairns, stays left of the creek until you reach its source at a tiny lake. Now you follow a broad crest, studded with alpine flowers in late July and August. This main southeast ridge provides a rocky route to the summit with its large cairn.

From the top, views extend in all directions—range after range merge into the distant blue. Be careful, however, on your return trip, especially if visibility is limited: the open ridges are somewhat featureless, so you must follow markers.

Fritillary butterfly on arnica— *G. J. Harris*

Rainclouds at the trailhead

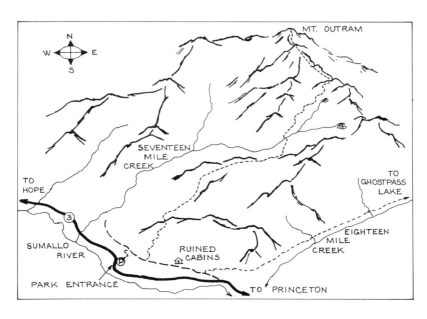

91 SILVERDAISY MOUNTAIN

Round trip 20 km (12.5 mi)
Allow 9 hours
High point 2051 m (6725 ft)
Elevation gain 1435 m (4700 ft)
Best July to September
Map Skagit 92H/3

There are two routes to this picturesque mountain area just west of Manning Park, one via a mine road and the other by the trail restored and maintained by dedicated volunteers. The second of these, though longer, is the more attractive as well as being more interesting historically, since it uses the old wagon road to the one-time aerial tram that was installed to remove the mineral wealth of Silverdaisy.

To reach the start of the trail from the west, turn right off Highway 3 to the Sumallo Grove picnic area 25.8 km (16 mi) east of its junction with Highway 5. From the parking area, walk south to the new (1987) footbridge across the Skagit River, then follow the old road for about 15 minutes to where the Silverdaisy Trail forks left from the main Skagit River Trail with which, so far, it has been sharing the route.

On this you start zigzagging upward, with seven switchbacks before you get clear of the main valley and swing east, high above the north side of Silverdaisy Creek. The next section is somewhat steeper and may be a little overgrown with alder. You have one or two rockslides to cross and at least one creek to negotiate over a collapsed bridge. Then you cut upward again to join an old jeep road coming in from the east, which brings you onto the cut made by the tramway from the old Invermay Mine. Stay with this road as

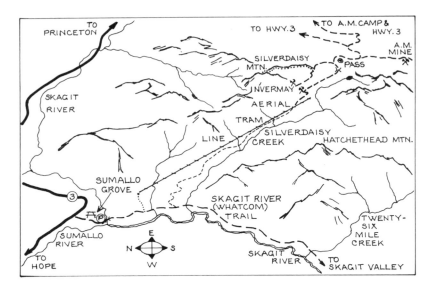

194

Silverdaisy Mountain from the north – *D. Ellis*

it rises to a pass (over which the road continues to the one-time A. M. Mine).

You, however, turn uphill left at the pass and, following the route across open meadow, rise gently to the summit with its panorama of mountain country, from Hatchethead almost due south, to the breathtaking sight of Mount Hozomeen farther away in the southeast, to the high country of the Cascade Divide with its peaks and deep tree-clad valleys.

You may, of course, make a crossover using the access road to the mine. To do so, leave one vehicle by the entrance to the mine road which goes off right (south) at the sign for Cayuse Flats, some 8.5 km (5 mi) east of the Sumallo Grove turnoff. When you return from the summit to the pass, follow the road downhill on the opposite side of the mountain from your ascent.

Looking north over the Punch Bowl

HOPE-MANNING PARK

92 PUNCH BOWL

Round trip (loop) 25.5 km (16 mi)
Allow 9 hours
High point 1784 m (5850 ft)
Elevation gain 1020 m (3350 ft)
Best July to September
Maps Skagit 92H/3, Hope 92H/6,
Princeton 92H/7

The drawback involved in making this a day trip is substantial: it gives you, like Moses, only a tantalizing glimpse of the land of promise. It is therefore best thought of as an overnight backpack, with a camp on the meadows just beyond the pass, or at the Punch Bowl itself. This gives you time to do some exploring, perhaps even make a trip to the north peak of Snass Mountain.

Difficulties with parking at the original trailhead have led to its replacement by one on the east side of Snass Creek, leaving Highway 3 on the left, 31.9 km (19.8 mi) beyond its divergence from Highway 5. Having passed Rhododendron Flats, move into the left lane to be ready for your turn a little beyond the bridge and on a corner. Drive the short distance into the parking area with its Dewdney Trail historic marker, then look left for the start of the new trail as it heads back towards the creek, which you cross to join the original. As you start off northward—staying west of the creek—you are stepping once more into B.C.'s colourful past, for this is the route of not one but two old trails, the Dewdney and the Whatcom. These remain together till the Whatcom follows the creek's east fork, but the Dewdney, using a lower pass, takes you into the valley of the north fork. That valley, ironically enough, is dry for much of its length, so much rock having been deposited on its floor that the stream flows underground for much of the year—there is even a genuine dry lake.

In warm weather, you should carry water, as there is none for some 6 km (3.5 mi) until you are fairly close to the pass. You may then enjoy the spectacular scenery at your leisure. The bold crags of Mount Dewdney are particularly fine, and in late summer the colours are a delight to the eye. The grade is not excessive, either, so only the closing in of the valley walls indicates that you are nearing the divide and the broad meadows of Paradise Valley beyond.

North of the pass the trail splits, with the main Dewdney Trail heading north and following the Tulameen River downstream across the meadows; it then veers northeast towards Whipsaw Creek and Princeton. More interesting, however, is the route going east on the Whatcom Trail to the Punch Bowl, the picturesque lake from which the Tulameen flows. The lake is 2.8 km (1.75 mi) from the fork and a short distance below Punch Bowl Pass, which lies to the south at a height of 1770 m (5800 ft).

From here you may return by your outward route, but it is now possible to continue south on the Whatcom Trail which runs along the sidehill below the pass and above the right bank of the east branch of the creek before zigzagging down to Snass Forks to rejoin the Dewdney Trail. Not only is it possible, it adds interest to travel to this lovely area by one historic trail and return by the other.

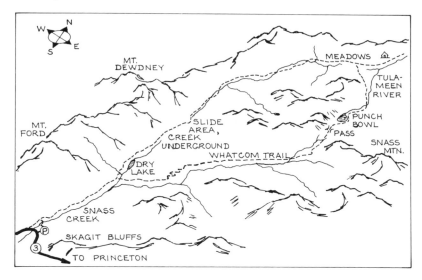

Coming into camp at Hope Pass

HOPE-MANNING PARK

93 HOPE PASS

Round trip (Hope Pass & return)
43 km (27 mi)
(Hope Pass/Nicomen Lake loop)
48 km (30 mi)
Allow 2 days or more
High point 1824 m (5980 ft)
Elevation gain 1035 m (3400 ft)
Best July to September
Maps Manning Park 92H/2,
   Princeton 92H/7

Not only does this delightful area provide a variety of hikes, ranging from one to three days in duration, the trail also gives you the chance to recreate in imagination some of B.C.'s colourful past, dating back to its building by Royal Engineers in the early 1860s. But that is not all its story; it remained a major packhorse road between Hope and Princeton until completion of Highway 3 in 1949 saw it fall into disuse.

For this trail, park at Cayuse Flats a short distance west of the bridge over Skaist Creek and 37.3 km (23 mi) east of the Highway 3 split from Highway 5. Cross to the north side of the road and follow the trail upstream to a log crossing of the creek, then head back uphill to the right to join the original trail. Now you travel parallel to and above the river on a good trail. If you are observant, you may still find old direction signs, relics of a more leisurely era. At 6.5 km (4 mi) comes a fork; the 9-km (5.6-mi) Park trail to Nicomen Lake via Grainger Creek goes off right, and yours crosses the creek and continues up the main valley. The little wilderness campsite just across the creek may be a destination for a short day hike, the round-trip distance being 14.5 km (9 mi).

198

Your next excitement comes in crossing the Skaist, which at present (1986) must be forded. From here on, you keep the river on your right as you gradually swing east and rise high above it, the trail rising by way of two zigzags—features that early travellers recorded. The pass itself is a broad meadow and provides a good camping spot, though cattle do graze in the area and may be a problem. From here, you may continue east, following Whipsaw Creek with its rough road and rejoining Highway 3 near Princeton. More rewarding, if you do not wish to return entirely by your original route, is the cross-country hike to Nicomen Lake, some 9 km (5.75 mi) to the south.

The rough trail to it goes off from the meadow just beyond the little creek that becomes the Skaist. Unfortunately it has become braided because of its use by range cattle; care is necessary—and probably a compass—to keep you heading more or less southward, passing a few pools as you travel through beautiful parklike surroundings. Next you lose some height as the trail takes you into forest. Then you must work uphill a little after crossing a small creek and making for the bold rock ridge slightly to your left, in front of which lies the lake with its wilderness campsite.

From here, the Park trail from Blackwall Peak (see Hike 95) brings you back down Grainger Creek valley to the fork. You stay high in the forest on the south side of its impressive canyon, crossing two tributaries and eventually descending by way of one or two switchbacks. This trip may be done in two days, but allow three if you can, so that you have time to explore around the lake before you return to the late-twentieth-century world.

Two notes: the trip to the lake is for experienced parties, and the Princeton map is inaccurate in its placing of Hope Pass.

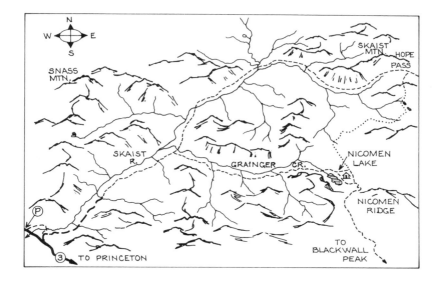

HOPE-MANNING PARK

94 POLAND LAKE

Round trip (from Allison Pass)
 18 km (11 mi)
Allow 7 hours

Round trip (from Gibson Pass)
 16 km (10 mi)
Allow 6 hours
High point 1754 m (5750 ft)
Elevation gain 410 m (1350 ft)
Best June to October
Map Manning Park 92H/2

This tree-fringed fishing lake enjoys not one but two approaches, one coming in from Allison Pass to the north, the other from the road to Gibson Pass to the east. As a result, the lake may be the destination of two hikes, or it may be a stop on a trip by parties who have left transportation at either end.

Allison Pass is some 48.5 km (30 mi) east of the junction of Highways 3 and 5. The Memaloose Trail heads southwest from behind the Department of Highways depot, which is on your right as you come from the Lower Mainland. This trail uses the creek valley of the same name (a tributary of the Similkameen). As an old trapper route, it remains in forest till it emerges at the lake's north end, from which you may walk along either shore to link up with the approach from the south.

Unfortunately there are indications that Parks and Outdoor Recreation hope to abandon responsibility for the old trail, despite its long history

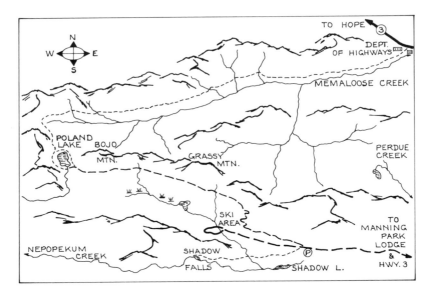

Hozomeen Mountain beyond the Skyline Trail

dating back into last century. However, such a trail does not deteriorate rapidly, and one can only hope that public interest will keep it in good condition.

The favoured route, a fire access road, begins from the parking spot at Strawberry Flats on the road from Manning Park Lodge to Gibson Pass, and gradually diverges to the right with a series of short switchbacks taking you to the ridge above the downhill ski area; generally, though, the grade is relatively gentle. For part of the way you are travelling through an extensively burned-over stretch of forest, the result of a fire in the 1940s, its slowly healing scars a silent reminder of the length of time needed for regeneration.

As you head west, you gradually work your way around the shoulder of the exotically named Bojo Mountain before descending to the lake with its wilderness campsite and shelter. One point: this trail is dry and it may be warm, so you should carry water for use en route.

HOPE-MANNING PARK

95 THREE BROTHERS MOUNTAIN

Round trip (to First Brother) 21 km (13 mi)
Allow 7 hours
High point 2273 m (7453 ft)
Elevation gain 320 m (1050 ft)
Best July to September
Map Manning Park 92H/2

Some obscure family scandal may be hinted at in the presence of a Fourth Brother, separate from and some distance north of the triple summits. However, as it is the smallest of the four, it may be ignored except by those who are not happy unless they reach the top of everything in sight.

Actually, the open alpine meadows over which you travel provide the most popular hiking country in Manning Park because of their easy accessibility and their flowers, abundant from about mid July into August. With this in mind, you will do well to camp near park headquarters or, better still, backpack in to Buckhorn wilderness campsite, so that you have the advantage of an early start to avoid the crowds.

To reach this delectable area, turn uphill from the north side of Highway 3 almost opposite Manning Park Lodge, passing the lookout with its parking area. Drive 4.8 km (3 mi) farther on a gravel road to Blackwell Peak parking lot, the end of the road. From here, several nature trails lead more or less north across the meadows, where a park naturalist is often on hand in season to lead nature walks and answer questions. Heather Trail is the best

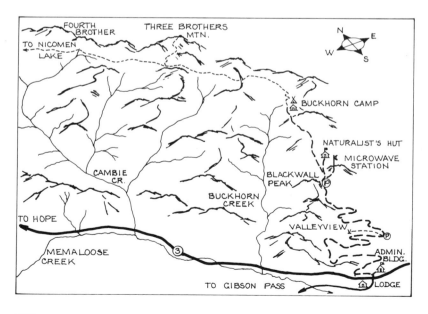

Hiking the Three Brothers Trail—*G. J. Harris*

one to follow for access to the Brothers; it gets its name from the abundance of that shrub around, though it is by no means the only plant you will see in season on these luxuriant meadows.

After you have passed Buckhorn camp, your trail skirts the west side of Big Buck Mountain. The Brothers are now close at hand—except the outcast—and it is perhaps fitting that the first is Big Brother, the highest. To reach the summit is easy; simply head upward east from the trail till you have only sky above and meadows and valleys below. From the top, its two slightly junior companions are close at hand, but one climb is sufficient for a day trip.

Note that if you are backpacking you may continue north on Heather Trail and reach Nicomen Ridge and the lake of the same name, with another primitive campsite beside it. From here, you may return or, if you wish, continue by trail down Grainger Creek to link up with Hope Pass Trail (Hike 93) at the Skaist River. Go south for a return to the main highway and the problem of getting back to your original parking lot, now a considerable distance away.

HOPE-MANNING PARK

96 LIGHTNING LAKES

Round trip 21 km (13 mi)
Allow 7 hours
High point 1150 m (4100 ft)
Elevation loss 100 m (325 ft)
Best May to October
Map Manning Park 92H/2

Although Lightning Lake itself and its neighbour, Flash, are well known even to casual visitors to Manning Park, you may penetrate farther into the valley and leave the crowds behind on the way to Strike and Thunder, the other two bodies of water that make up the chain. You may even do some fishing in Strike Lake (which is reputed to contain trout), especially if you make this an overnight trip and stay in the wilderness campsite by the lake.

Your parking spot is in the Lightning Lakes Day Use Area, which you reach by forking left off the Gibson Pass road a little over 3 km (2 mi) west of Manning Park Lodge. From here, cross the dam at the head of the lake and proceed west, passing the Frosty Mountain trailhead en route. As you turn south, you come to a footbridge across the narrows that gives access to the trail along the opposite shore, permitting a choice of routes. Next comes Flash Lake, with trails on either side also. From its western end, however, you should stay on the north side of the creek for the third member of the quartet, Strike Lake, with its hypothetical trout population.

Somewhat removed from the others and a little lower in the valley is Thunder Lake, some 3 km (2 mi) beyond. Here the enclosing slopes are steep, making this lake an eerie place even in summer; in winter and spring it is best avoided altogether because of the danger of snowslides. If on a backpacking trip, you may leave your gear in the wilderness campsite at the far end of Strike Lake and walk along the trail up Lightning Creek to its end at the outlet from Thunder Lake, a dark, lonely spot.

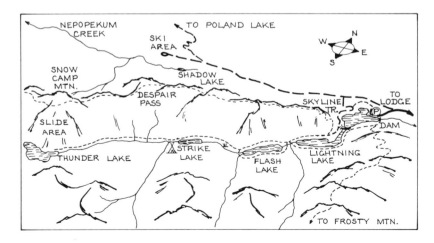

Lightning Lake from the dam

This hike differs from most others in that your high point is at its start; remember, therefore, if you are making this a one-day trip, that your return is uphill.

HOPE-MANNING PARK

97 FROSTY MOUNTAIN

Round trip (loop) 24 km (15 mi)
Allow 10 hours

Round trip (direct) 21 km (13 mi)
Allow 8 hours
High point 2410 m (7900 ft)
Elevation gain 1150 m (3900 ft)
Best July to September
Map Manning Park 92H/2

With alternative routes now possible, you have the choice of returning as you went out or making a crossover of this hike to the highest point in Manning Park. The hiker may now ascend from Lightning Lake; or use the longer trail that forks right from the fire access road leading to Windy Joe Mountain; or make a loop trip, perhaps with an overnight stopover en route.

From Manning Park Lodge, drive west to the parking lot at the Lightning Lakes Day Use Area, cross the dam and start on the trail southward along the east shore. Very shortly the Frosty Mountain trail diverges to the left, rising steeply in a series of switchbacks on the north flank of the mountain for nearly 7 km (4.5 mi) to a campsite. After this, the trail heads up over country that becomes progressively more open, with large broken rock for you to negotiate. A short distance below the summit, the trail from the Windy Joe side joins from the left and the final 400 m (1300 ft) is a scramble to the first peak, the objective for hikers.

Possibilities for the return will already have presented themselves. If you have organized a second car to be in Beaver Pond parking lot east of Park

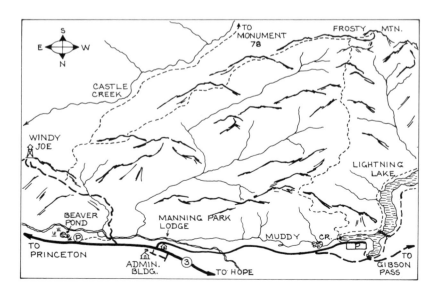

Frosty Mountain from the trail — *R. Latham*

Headquarters, you may return by the Windy Joe Trail during the season when the "summer only" bridge is in place over a branch of the Similkameen River near the end of the hike. On the other hand, return by the trail to Lightning Lake gives spectacular views over the lakes, up Gibson Pass, along the Skyline Trail, and across to the meadows to the north of Highway 3.

A glimpse of Thunder Lake below Hozomeen Mountain— *D. Ellis*

HOPE-MANNING PARK

98 SKYLINE TRAIL EAST

Round trip (loop) 17.5 km (10.8 mi)
Allow 7 hours
High point 1995 m (6550 ft)
Elevation gain 775 m (2550 ft)

Round trip (Camp Mowich)
24 km (15 mi)
Allow 10 hours or overnight
High point 1920 m (6300 ft)
Elevation gain 550 m (1800 ft)
Best July to October
Map Manning Park 92H/2

For the hiker in Manning Park, the Skyline Trail offers several exciting possibilities: first, a circular tour starting on Lightning Lake or at Strawberry Flats the Gibson Pass Divide, a possibility that exists because the original trail from Spruce Bay was cut off for a time by the damming of Lightning Lake and a replacement was provided from farther west; second, a backpack westward to Camp Mowich with the option of returning to your point of departure or of completing the crossover to the Skagit Valley (Hike 77).

To reach the Lightning Lake trailhead, drive west along the Gibson Pass road, forking left for the Day use Area and parking near the dam about 4 km (2.5 mi) from Highway 3 at Manning Park Lodge. You set out initially by crossing to the south side of the lake, recrossing by the footbridge at the narrows to the north bank, then forking right from the trail along the lakes after a total of about 25 minutes from the start. Now comes your climb to the long high ridge on which you will travel to the Strawberry Flats Trail junction just before Despair Pass. On your way along this south-facing ridge with its meadows—beautiful but fragile—you are regaled with the sight of Hozomeen Mountain standing proudly to the southwest over the lake chain below.

At the junction, you go right for the descent to the Flats, noting that this north-facing slope dries out later in the summer than the one you have left. If you have been able to leave a second car at the parking lot, your hike ends at the road, a short distance after you join the Three Falls Trail, for a 13-km (8-mi) trip; otherwise, you must continue downhill parallel with the road for an extra 4.5 km (2.8 mi).

If you are planning a round trip to Camp Mowich or the crossover, the Strawberry Flats starting point makes a shorter hike with less climbing. For this approach, drive west on the Gibson Pass road for 7 km (4.5 mi) to park at the trailhead, then set off west downstream on Nepopekum Creek, before branching left (south) and heading for the ridge while the Three Falls Trail continues straight ahead. Once on the ridge, a right turn at the junction with the original Skyline Trail is followed by a drop into Despair Pass, but soon you are regaining height to pass Snow Camp and Lone Goat on their south sides, both mountains showing signs of the damage caused by random hikers straying from the trail.

Now, once again, you lose height as you make your way westward to the wilderness campsite at Mowich Creek, a spot from which the backpacker may enjoy a variety of walks on the transverse ridge or continue the crossover to the Skagit.

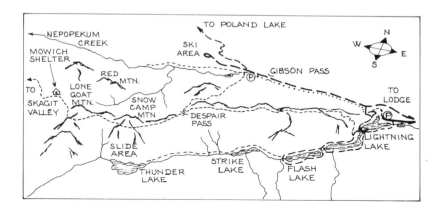

99 CRATER MOUNTAIN

Round trip 26 km (16 mi)
Allow 10 hours
High point 2294 m (7522 ft)
Elevation gain 1586 m (5200 ft)
Best June to October
Map Ashnola 92H/1

Should you be staying in the Ashnola valley, you may add this leg-stretcher to other hikes in the area, spring and fall being the times most favoured. The route described, though along an old road that is drivable for some distance, is probably best followed on foot to enjoy the views as they unfold and to avoid the nuisance of having to clear off the rocks that have tumbled down from the cutbank on the uphill side of the track.

For access to the valley, turn off Highway 3 about 3 km (1.9 mi) west of Keremeos. Next you cross the one-time Great Northern Railway span over the Similkameen (from which all subsequent distances are taken) and turn south, crossing to the river's west bank after some 10 km (6.2 mi). This outing then begins 8 km (5 mi) beyond the latter crossing and just below the Ashnola Wildlife Management cabin, where a range road forks right and uphill then bends back to encounter its first gate, with possible parking nearby. From here, you rise quite steeply to cross Crater Creek on another corner, then continue to reach the bench level, with views across to the peaks of Cathedral Provincial Park. Your next stage is over parklike country, a pair of old sod cabins to the left of your route mute witnesses to an attempt at homesteading.

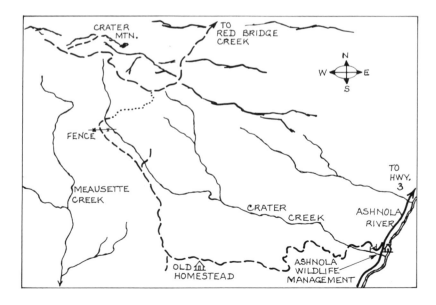

Clouds drifting over Crater Mountain

Still on the road, you now traverse an open slope, brilliant with blooms in early summer, intolerably hot in the high season, but bordered with pale gold aspen contrasting with the greens of the spruce and pine in the fall. And now you swing back left into the upper valley of Crater Creek's west branch as you cross a cattle grid and the forest begins to close in.

Another gate follows (don't forget to close it) and you continue rising, staying left at a fork and remaining on the creek's south side till the road, as such, comes to an end, leaving you with a trail used by both hikers and cattle, as is pretty obvious. Yet another gate follows, the route acquires a mixture of blue and orange tapes, and finally crosses the creek near its source. Although you are soon in the open again, you are faced with a mess of braided cattle trails in the meantime, so keep working up to the right and towards the head of yet another branch of Crater Creek. Follow this watercourse uphill, your objective now in front of you as you emerge on open meadows once more. Head across these to an old road, on which you go left as far as a right fork leading to the summit with its cairn, its all-round views and its interesting geological formations.

Ladyslipper Lake

KEREMEOS

100 CATHEDRAL LAKES

Allow for Ewart Creek (one-way)
10 hours
High Trail (one-way) 6.5 hours
Wall Creek (one-way) 8 hours
Best mid July to September
Map Ashnola 92H/1

Three approaches—four if you include the tourist jeep road—will take you from the Ashnola valley to this high country wonderland set in the midst of Cathedral Provincial Park. Each hiking trail, too, has its own qualities and features, leaving to you the choice amongst them, though, of course, you can combine at least two in a crossover with a car at each end.

Of the routes, the Ewart Creek Trail starts farthest downstream and goes highest. High Trail, ironically, is the lowest of the three and suffers by contrast with the other two because it never gets above the treeline and so lacks their views. The Wall Creek Trail, beginning farthest upstream and forming part of the Centennial Trail, is midway between the others in altitude, but like the Ewart Creek approach rises into open alpine country before descending to the campground at Quiniscoe Lake.

For the Ewart Creek Trail, cross back to the east bank of the Ashnola 15 km (9.3 mi) from the Similkameen bridge, and on the single-lane dirt road proceed upstream for another 3.4 km (2.2 mi) to its end at a wooden hut. Cross the creek on a log bridge and head south, first on a jeep road but soon forking left on a trail, one needing no Sherlock Holmes to deduce that it is used by cattle and horses as well as humans.

Next you recross the creek, merge with the Centennial Trail soon after, and continue on the east bank before going back to the west bank and starting to climb, not inappropriately, given that you are now following Mountain

Goat Creek. The cairned route finally crests at nearly 2500 m (8200 ft) on the west shoulder of Lakeview Mountain for an altitude gain of some 1710 m (5600 ft) before you drop into the valley of Lakeview Creek to face the final rise to Quiniscoe Lake, 23 km (14.5 mi) from the start.

High Trail begins at a parking lot and campsite nearly 23 km (14 mi) from the Similkameen, just under 2 km (1.2 mi) beyond the private jeep road. To begin, you cross the Ashnola on a smart footbridge, climb to intersect the road, returning to the road later for the crossing of Lakeview Creek. Thereafter, the trail heads off on its own, crossing Lindsey Creek and ultimately meeting with the high-country Diamond Loop and Cathedral Rim trails in short order as you descend to the campground, following a hike of 14.5 km (9 mi), your height gain this time being only 1375 m (4500 ft).

For the third option, you must drive almost 50 km (31 mi) upriver to a parking spot marked with a Centennial Trail sign. Once more you begin with a river crossing, this time on a slightly tipsy-looking bridge, then you head downstream until you reach the Wall Creek crossing, from which time you stay on its north side, eventually swinging away from the main creek in favour of an unnamed tributary. As you ascend, the forest becomes more scattered, and finally you reach the alpine, your route marked with stone cairns as you head for the col (your high point).

Actually, because you start higher on this trail, the elevation change, 1160 m (3800 ft), is not as great as you might have expected, given that you rise to 2330 m (7650 ft) at the pass. Beyond here you meet the Cathedral Rim Trail for the final descent into camp, after a trip of almost 20 km (12.5 mi).

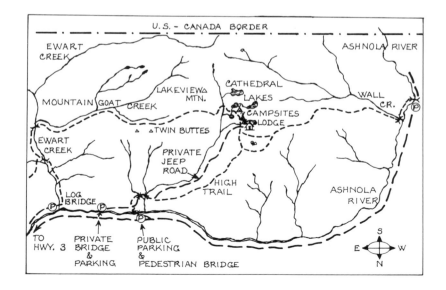

213

Smokey the Bear facing the storm

KEREMEOS

101 CATHEDRAL RIM

Round trip (south end) 11 km (7 mi)
Allow 6 hours
High point 2614 m (8570 ft)
Elevation gain 540 m (1770 ft)

Round trip (north end) 10 km (6 mi)
Allow 5 hours
High point 2553 m (8369 ft)
Elevation gain 480 m (1570 ft)
Best July to September
Map Ashnola 92H/1

Setting aside valley-bottom walks around the lakes in Cathedral Provincial Park or minor circular outings such as Diamond Circuit, two major hikes are ascents of the above named and Lakeview Mountain, their order determined by these considerations: should the weather break—a not unheard of thing in the mountains—Cathedral Rim offers the greater variety, and the hike (or hikes) on it may be expanded or contracted depending on the access chosen.

Of such approaches, the one via Glacier Lake comes closest to splitting the complete hike into two more or less equal parts, the one to the north giving a high-level circle route over Quiniscoe (formerly Bomford) Mountain and Red, while the southern segment, after an ascent to the summit of Pyramid Mountain, is notable for a variety of geological features that it brings within reach. But first you must reach the headwall above the lake, and to do so you may begin on the Pyramid Lake Trail from the campsite, then fork right for Glacier Lake to emerge into the open by the outlet. Alternatively, you may start along the south side of Quiniscoe Lake itself, following a trail that angles upward to cross the ridge separating the two valleys, then joins the main trail above Glacier Lake.

The ascent to the Rim is quite steep, over broken rock in its later stages, with cairns marking the route. Once at the pass you have the options: left for Pyramid Mountain, right for Quiniscoe. If the former is your choice, you follow cairns to the summit for your first all-round view, noting as you proceed the abundance of animal sign and perhaps seeing some of the creatures themselves. Then as you continue southeast you reach your first point of geological interest, Devil's Woodpile, a large outcropping of columnar basalt, followed shortly by Stone City, piled-up rounded rocks like giant curling stones.

Next you note a trail dropping off left to Ladyslipper Lake, your last safe descent to the basin. There are, however, other natural wonders to admire before you retrace your steps to this point, notably Smokey the Bear and the Giant Cleft. The former demands no exercise of fancy to see the rock's

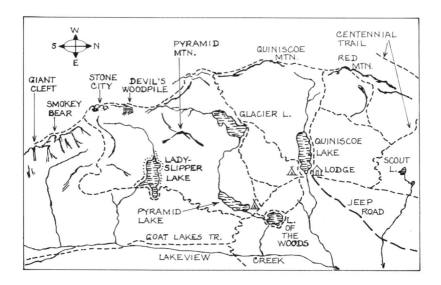

resemblance to the forest-fire fighter, the latter impresses even the least imaginative with its dizzying height. To reach the last-named feature does demand a little scrambling, perfectly simple when the surface is dry but a little tricky perhaps when snow is on the ground and the rocks are slippery.

From here you should probably retrace your steps to the Ladyslipper Lake Trail, leaving Grimface Mountain to the climbers. Down to the lake is perfectly straightforward, providing views of Smokey in reverse and the Cleft from below and passing through several groves of larch, their delicate golden needles beautiful on a fine fall day. At the lake, you make your way around the southeastern shore before rising over the transverse ridge that separates Ladyslipper from Pyramid Lake and returning to Quiniscoe by the main lakes trail.

Reverting to your arrival at the pass above Glacier Lake, had you gone right, you would have followed a cairned route over Quiniscoe Mountain, cresting at 2250 m (7380 ft), with one possible return via the pass above Quiniscoe Lake, an interesting descent with the last vestiges of a glacier on your right, followed by an alpine meadow, the talus to the left shrill with marmots. Next you drop to the lake's west end and your journey along its north side back to camp for a trip of 8 km (5 mi). However, instead of returning directly, you may follow the route (rough and rocky in places and marked only by cairns) over Red Mountain, descending to join first the Centennial Trail from Wall Creek, then High and Scout Lake Trails as you approach the end of your journey.

And, if your time in the park is limited, a traverse of the whole rim from end to end can be achieved in one long but rewarding day—especially if the weather gods smile—by ascending by the Ladyslipper route and descending on the Centennial Trail, or vice versa.

Stone City

The Giant Cleft

Last fork before the summit

102 LAKEVIEW MOUNTAIN

Round trip (direct) 11 km (6.8 mi)
Allow 6 hours

Round trip (loop) 13 km (8 mi)
Allow 8 hours
High point 2630 m (8622 ft)
Elevation gain 555 m (1820 ft)
Best July to September
Map Ashnola 92H/1

Assuming that the weather has held, you may make this summit the high point (but only literally) of your stay in Cathedral Provincial Park, the more so since you have to go down 170 m (550 ft) into the valley of Lakeview Creek before you even begin your hike up the mountain's north slopes, your route at first following the Centennial Trail as it leaves for Ewart Creek.

At the outset, you follow the main trail past Pyramid Lake, then take the left fork for Goat Lake and the Centennial Trail just beyond the creek crossing. Now comes the steady descent which you continue after another left fork, where the right leads to Goat Lake. Finally, at Lakeview Creek, you

Lakeview Mountain as seen from Cathedral Rim

reach the low point and start rising again, crossing some rather wet meadowy sections with the help of two long catwalks. Then after 20 minutes or so you approach a creek which you follow uphill on its south side while the trees thin out and the bare slopes of Lakeview appear ahead. Soon you reach your last fork: left for the Centennial Trail, right for Lakeview. Here, too, you are suddenly in open alpine country with cairns of generous size keeping you on the right track for the summit. From this lofty eminence you look over the Cathedral Lakes in the valley to the west, to the peaks of Cathedral Ridge in the southwest and to the nearby squarish-looking mountain, appropriately called the Boxcar, to the south.

Your return may simply reverse your outward journey; however, if you are an experienced hiker and have good weather, you may turn this into a crossover by continuing south slightly to the east of the ridge crest, down into the saddle between Lakeview and the Boxcar, then dropping through the firs and larches to reach the Goat Lakes Trail about 400 metres from the outlet. The short trip back to the lakes is well worthwhile, their situation in the narrow steep valley being quite dramatic. Thereafter, you follow the park trail back through the meadows on the valley bottom to the Lakeview fork, where you keep left for your final trudge uphill to camp. Even here, however, a small detour may provide variety for the expenditure of no more than five minutes additional time. For this, go right towards Lake of the Woods immediately after crossing the outlet from Pyramid Lake, and once there, stay left for your return to Quiniscoe Lake after passing along its west shore, from which you get a fine last view of the mountain you have just conquered.

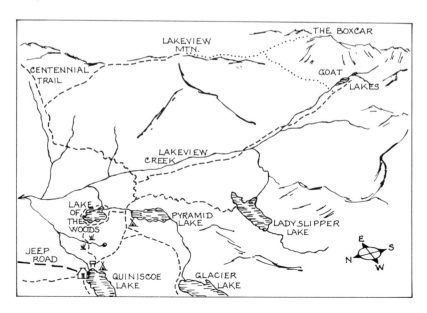

103 KEREMEOS COLUMNS

Round trip 12 km (7.5 mi)
Allow 5 hours
High point 1205 m (3950 ft)
Elevation gain 717 m (2350 ft)
Best May to November
Map Keremeos 92E/4

Surface instances of columnar basalt, the result of bygone igneous activity, are not all that rare; such striking examples as these 100-m (325-ft) pillars, however, are sufficiently out of the ordinary to justify their having been designated a Provincial Park, even if, by a nice irony, some mistake in surveying has the feature in private property. In any event, the visitor to Keremeos should try to include the hike over the open sagebrush range to these natural curiosities.

From the junction of Highways 3 and 3A east of Keremeos, travel the Penticton road for 3.3 km (2 mi), turn right just beyond the cemetery and drive to where the public road ends at a gate, a house to the left. This is the home of the Clifton family, and the hike is across their property, so your second move is to ask permission to proceed up the old forest access road, now a cattle route (your first was to park clear of the gate). The family has always been quite happy to allow hiking, so you will repay their courtesy by leaving all gates as you find them, three of them including the one by the house.

Once on foot, you start switchbacking upward on the open slope, hot work in the summer sunshine, so this hike is best early or late in the year, when the heat is tempered somewhat. You will need water, too, as there is none en route, but the rewards for setting out are many: striking views of the Similkameen valley, its varying shades of green contrasting with the bare rock ridges and the golden brown slopes.

At the top of an S-bend, you start swinging around the end of the ridge, a rocky knoll with TV towers above you on your left. Gradually you rise towards it, passing on the east, and noting that the steep south face is a mask for the gentle approach from the north. Now you begin to turn eastward, towards a watercourse, Armstrong Creek, an intermittent stream which, however, you do not cross, taking instead the left fork where the road splits, the

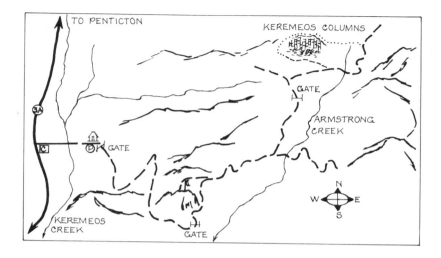

paler green of a cluster of aspen ahead of you by the creek contrasting with the surrounding conifers.

By this time, after another fork, to the right this time, you can see glimpses of the columns above to the left, and finally, where the road goes straight on to cross the creek, you cut back to emerge at their base, the tumbled remains of others showing how much more extensive the whole exposure must have been at one time. If you wish to look down upon the scene from above, start near the big Douglas-fir to the left and clamber up to the small cairn from which you may survey Keremeos, its surroundings, and the high Alpine to the southeast, its white peaks attesting to the snow-fall that it may receive in almost any month of the year.

Your return is by the same route, and now you may appreciate again the distant views down the valley of the Similkameen beyond the sage-clothed slopes, perhaps paying a visit to the TV-towered knoll en route to look over Keremeos and westward up the valley.

ADDITIONAL HIKES

For these, use the relevant maps plus information from Forest Service, Provincial Parks or other local sources and make your own way; only the approaches are given.

1. SECHELT
Mount Elphinstone (92G/5): Travel 5.5 km (3.4 mi) north from the Langdale ferry terminal on the Port Mellon road. Go left on a gravel road, one branch of which circles the mountain from the north.

Panther Peak (92G/5, G/12): Midway between McNair Creek and Port Mellon, a 4WD logging road goes off west following the creek's north side to McNair Lake, from which a rough route heads east to the peak.

Mount Hallowell (92G/12): Take a logging road to the right about 100 metres west of Pender Harbour School, some 64 km (40 mi) west of Langdale ferry terminal.

2. HOWE SOUND–PEMBERTON
Mountain Lake (92G/11): Go right off Highway 99 in Britannia Beach village just north of the mining museum. Cross the creek, park at the barrier 1.4 km (0.9 mi) from the highway and follow the old road upstream.

Shannon Falls (92G/11): From the parking lot, go upstream towards the falls and watch for a taped route on the opposite bank a little before the waterwheel.

Mount Mulligan (92G/11): Go right off Highway 99 just beyond the Stawamus Chief on the Stawamus River logging road. Drive to a fork about 7 km (4.4 mi) from the highway, and park. Go right on the older road.

Brohm Ridge (92G/14): Just over 3.3 km (2.1 mi) north of the Alice Lake Park exit from Highway 99, turn sharp right on an old logging road which forks after 900 metres. Both branches eventually lead to the ridge.

Tricouni Meadows (92G/14): Turn west off Highway 99 to cross the Cheakamus River 21 km (13.1 mi) north of Alice Lake Park exit. Turn left after the railway crossing and drive to a gate just before a major fork. Go right for about 1 km (0.6 mi), then left on a marked trail.

Brew Mountain via Brandywine Creek (92J/3): Park as for Hike 37 but take the left fork, cross the creek, and from the right fork beyond, head for the Brew divide.

Owl Lakes (92J/7): From the D'Arcy road (Hike 44), turn off left on a dirt road about 11 km (7 mi) north of Mount Currie and just beyond the Owl Creek Forest Recreation Site.

3. LOWER FRASER VALLEY
Blue Mountain (92G/1, G/8): Go left off Dewdney Trunk Road on McNutt Road 3 km (2 mi) beyond the store at Webster's Corners and head for a parking area a short distance beyond the B.C. Hydro powerhouse.

Mount Crickmer (92G/8): From the Dewdney Trunk Road east of Haney, turn left on a gravel road just west of Stave Lake for 6.4 km (4 mi). Park at a gate just after a right fork to a correctional institution.

Lucky-Four Mine (92H/4): Turn right off Highway 1 at the Jones Lakes exit about 40 km (25 mi) east of Chilliwack. Drive south along the lake's east side and fork left on an old logging road after 3 km (2 mi).

4. CHILLIWACK RIVER
Slesse Mountain Trail (92H/4): After crossing the Slesse Creek bridge about 20 km (13.5 mi) east of Vedder Crossing on the Chilliwack Lake Road, go right on the logging road up the east side of the creek for 6 km (3.7 mi), cross back to the west bank and continue upstream, staying left at all forks for 3.6 km (2.2 mi). Park and recross to the east bank (old bridge still in place, October 1986), going right briefly to find the trail on the left side of the old road.

Red Mountain Mine (92H/4): See above. Stay right at the final fork, 3.3 km (2 mi) from the crossing to the west bank.

Mount Mercer (92H/4): For the approach to the T-junction at Foley Creek, see Hike